Chapters on Interdisciplinary Research and Research Skills

Chapters on Interdisciplinary Research and Research Skills

Koen van der Gaast

Machiel Keestra (ed.)

Laura Koenders

Steph Menken (ed.)

Ger Post

Amsterdam University Press

Chapters on Interdisciplinary Research and Research Skills is part of the Series Perspectives on Interdisciplinarity.

This book is a special edition, compiled for to the MSc Course Research Methodologies as taught at the Faculty of Aerospace Engineering at Delft University of Technology.

The first part consists of chapters from *An Introduction to Interdisciplinary Research,* Steph Menken and Machiel Keestra (eds) (2016), ISBN 9789462981843. Authors are Lucas Rutting, Ger Post, Machiel Keestra, Mieke de Roo, Sylvia Blad and Linda de Greef.

The second part consists of chapters from *Academic Skills for Interdisciplinary Studies, revised edition,* Koen van der Gaast, Laura Koenders and Ger Post (2019), 9789463720922. This book was originally published as *Academische vaardigheden voor interdisciplinaire studies* by Joris J.W. Buis, Ger Post and Vincent R. Visser (2015). Now available as *Academische vaardigheden voor interdisciplianire studies. Vierde, herziene druk,* by Koen van der Gaast, Laura Koenders and Ger Post (2019), 9789463725118. Translation: Vivien Collingwood.

Cover and interior design: Matterhorn Amsterdam

ISBN   978 94 6372 825 6
e-ISBN   978 90 4855 397 6 (pdf)
NUR   143

© Koen van der Gaast, Machiel Keestra, Laura Koenders, Steph Menken, Ger Post / Amsterdam University Press B.V., Amsterdam 2020

Contents

Part 1
From
'An Introduction
to Interdisciplinary
Research'

1 Introduction

Half a century ago, philosopher of science Karl Popper (1963) famously observed: "We are not students of some subject matter, but students of problems. And problems may cut right across the boundaries of any subject matter or discipline." This statement has become increasingly relevant. Today, many of the phenomena and problems that we are trying to understand and solve indeed 'cut across' the traditional boundaries of academic disciplines. Modern technological developments and globalization add to the complexity of problems and, in response, we are becoming increasingly aware that an integrated approach is necessary. Healthcare, climate change, food security, energy, financial markets, and quality of life are but a few examples of subjects that drive scientists to 'cross borders' and engage with experts from multiple fields to find solutions. In short, complex questions and problems necessitate an interdisciplinary approach to research.

Most real-life problems are multifaceted, in that they have multiple types of causes and determining factors. These different types of causes and determining factors often have to be addressed in different ways with different disciplinary methods. We know from research, for example, that alcohol intake is involved in over half of the violent acts that take place in the public domain. However, the relationship between the intake of alcohol and aggressive behavior is much more complex, and different disciplines have different perspectives on this relationship, as you can see in figure 1. Each discipline's focus is on another factor (in this case either nurture- of nature-related) at a different level of analysis, using different theoretical frameworks, and different methodologies.

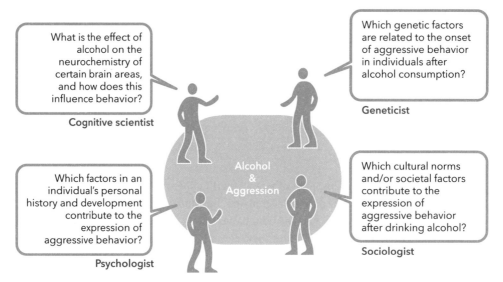

Figure 1   Different perspectives on the relationship between alcohol intake and aggression

Another example of a multifaceted problem is the financial crisis. Over the past five years, academics from different disciplines have tried to explain what caused the global economic recession. These disciplinary explanations, however, only shed light on part of the problem. When combined, they may offer a more comprehensive explanation, as you can see below in figure 2.

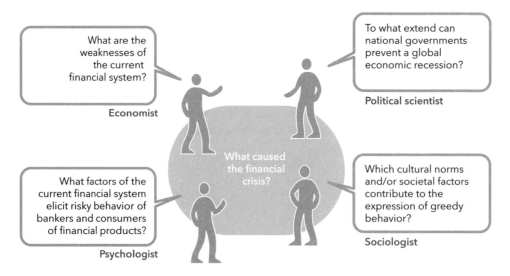

Figure 2   Different perspectives on the causes of the financial crisis

The previous examples illustrate that knowledge is, to a large extent, generated within separate disciplines (see also box 1). Consequently, in interdisciplinary research we need these disciplines to provide insights into different aspects of our research problem. So, before we turn the focus to interdisciplinarity, it is essential to understand what an academic discipline is. For this, it is useful to understand the origins of academic disciplines, as well as their development. In the following chapter, we define the academic discipline before providing an overview of the discipline's inception and expansion throughout the science system and beyond. This is followed by a definition of the concept of interdisciplinarity and important related concepts (chapter 4). Chapter 5 focuses on the importance of complexity as the driving force behind interdisciplinarity, and provides an overview of the different manifestations of complexity. Finally, chapter 6 provides a description of the integration of disciplinary knowledge to produce new, interdisciplinary insights (see the example below on an interdisciplinary theory on poverty), which is the key feature of interdisciplinary research.

Box 1
An interdisciplinary theory on poverty

Eldar Shafir and Sendhil Mullainathan, respectively Professor of Psychology at Princeton and Professor of Economics at Harvard, developed an interdisciplinary theory on poverty. Their theory, published in the book *Scarcity – Why Having Too Little Means So Much*, was praised both in and outside academia.

The starting point for their research was the finding that poor people generally make bad decisions. Compared to middle-class people, poor people eat less healthily (even when healthy food is made available to them), take out loans with high interest rates more often, and are generally bad at taking long-term effects into consideration. However, as Shafir said: "No one was studying why poor people are making these bad decisions" (E. Shafir, pers. comm., 12 December 2013).

Shafir and Mullainathan started to connect findings from their disciplines. They found that the bad decisions poor people make are actually well researched in psychology. For example, poor people were discounting the future and showed loss aversion in their decisions, two effects known from research on decision-making. The question the researchers then investigated was: Why are poor people more prone to these effects than others?

▼

In their experiments, they found that psychological traits like bad character or low intelligence could not explain why poor people made more bad decisions than people with more financial resources. Instead, Shafir and Mullainathan came up with another explanation: It is often a person's context that dictates whether someone can make a good decision. Shafir again: "Slowly came the realization that many of the mistakes made by the poor are caused by poverty itself."

In their book, the researchers explain that when someone experiences scarcity - whether it is a lack of money, friends or time - this shortage 'captures' that person's mind. Her mind will intentionally and unintentionally deal with scarcity, and this leaves less cognitive capacity for other things, such as making a good decision.

2 What is science?
A brief philosophy of science

2.1 What is science?

In the previous chapter we quoted philosopher of science Karl Popper, who contended that solving a problem often requires the integration of insights that pertain to different subject matters or disciplines. Popper observes a certain tension between the way that scientific disciplines are organized and how problems present themselves. Indeed, interdisciplinary research is a way to overcome this tension and to organize scientific research in such a way that it is not impeded by the organizational structure of the sciences itself. Since it is important to understand both the value and the limitations of this organizational structure, we need to briefly reflect on what science is and does. In other words: let us reflect on some basic ingredients of science, the way philosophers of science do. There are many ingredients that appear to be familiar enough, though perhaps not easy to understand, such as theory, concept, fact, hypothesis, explanation, inference, induction, deduction, and so on. Given the limitations of this handbook, we will only pay attention to a few of these and recommend you to look elsewhere for a more comprehensive introduction to the philosophy of science.

Scientists work hard to understand the world or reality, in much the same way as lay persons do. In fact, scientists cannot help but do this by building on the same pillars as we all have to. They have to rely upon sense perception in order to draw upon information about the world available and they have to use reasoning in order to draw the right conclusions about this information and to avoid mistakes. Nonetheless, if one reads scientific texts, it immediately becomes apparent that there are striking differences between scientific and lay efforts to reach an understanding of reality. Scientists do not usually rely on just their senses as lay persons do, but rather use a variety of instruments to perceive more, smaller, larger, and different objects than lay persons do: microscopes, structured interviews, telescopes, fMRI scanners, validated questionnaires, participatory observations, archive research, and so on. Similarly, their reasoning and arguments are often quite different from those of lay persons, as they work with rather specific concepts, propositions, formulas, figures, tables, and schemes and tend to strictly follow the laws of logic in connecting those. Put differently, they work with large and complex collections of symbols, all arranged in a quite particular structure.

Apart from the fact that scientists rely upon sense perception and reasoning in ways that are not common to the average lay person, but use quite specific instruments and methods, there is another fact that is peculiar to how scientists operate. One of the greatest scientists, Isaac Newton, once wrote in a letter to a colleague that "If I have seen further, it is by standing on the shoulders of giants." This remark reflects how scientists build upon each other's work, aim to put each other's work to the test, to expand the knowledge that others have produced, to use that knowledge in new applications, or to prove that their colleague's conclusions are not correct and that adjustments are required. In other words, much more than lay persons, a scientist is expected to be well informed about the relevant insights, results, instruments, and methods that other scientists have been and are using – relevant for answering the questions that the scientist is asking. Obviously, what is relevant for answering a particular question is often not easy to determine: a connection to a previously-held irrelevant factor might be established when new research has been executed and new instruments and methods have been developed, for example.

Employing highly elaborate forms of sense perception and reasoning, and building upon the relevant work of other scientists: these are important features that distinguish the scientists' acquisition of knowledge from the way lay persons operate. We can elucidate these features by looking at the figure below, which presents what is called the 'empirical cycle' or the 'Science Cycle': a process that represents how scientists go about when acquiring knowledge.

2.2 Moving through the Science Cycle

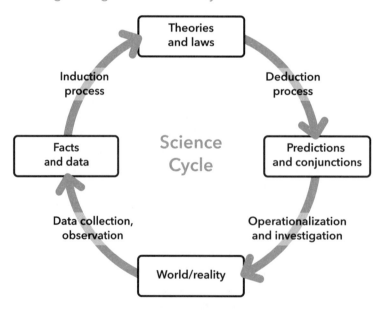

Figure 3   The Science Cycle, consisting of four processes, connecting four components – together providing a (somewhat simplified) representation of science as an ongoing process. Note that reasoning and sense perception are present, albeit in specific ways.

Theories and laws

The top of the Science Cycle (figure 3) consists of the most important component of science; that is to say, theories and laws. A theory consists of concepts, principles, ideas, or statements that together provide a comprehensive background or framework within which other ingredients of science are located. Familiar examples of theories are the theory of relativity, the theory of evolution, the behaviorist theory of learning, the structuralist theory of meaning, or the theory of plate tectonics.

In general, a theory offers a framework that usually captures the result of years of studies by numerous scientific colleagues, who have accumulated a wealth of facts and insights into a particular phenomenon. The theory offers elements that can be used to explain and predict phenomena that belong to the scope of the theory. If phenomena are complex, such as cognitive or social phenomena, it is likely that multiple theories are applicable to specific features of such phenomena: genetic, developmental, social, and geographical features might all be somehow relevant and might require interdisciplinary integration for a robust prediction and explanation, as we will learn in part 2. It is important to realize that there is a difference between the areas of research with regard to the prevalence and importance of specific theories. Physics is dominated by a few theories and a host of specific laws connected to those theories, while in the social sciences and humanities there are many competing theories but also many insights that have not been published in terms of a 'theory'. Given the fact that social, cultural, and historical phenomena are very complex and dynamic, this lesser prominence of theories in those domains should not be surprising, as such phenomena can usually be partly elucidated from multiple perspectives.

In many – though not in all – cases, we consider laws as part of a theory: for example, the law of gravity and several laws of motion belong to the theory of classical mechanics formulated by Newton. Somewhat differently, the Mendelian laws of inheritance are now part of the theory of classical genetics. Note that laws of inheritance have a probabilistic character, which distinguishes them from laws from classical mechanics and many other laws. Indeed, in the life, the social, and the human sciences such probabilistic laws are more prevalent because of the more multi-causal nature of phenomena in their domains. This also underlines the importance of distinguishing between correlative relations and causal relations: as long as we do not really know what causal mechanisms are involved, we should be cautious about interpreting probabilistic relations.

Deduction and developing predictions & conjunctions

As mentioned earlier, besides sense perception, reasoning is crucial for scientists, and deduction and induction are the most prominent reasoning processes involved in science. A scientist who wants to add to a body of knowledge will start by offering new predictions from a particular theory, or from the combination of two different theories – predictions that have, until now, not been formulated or tested. Such predictions are formulated by a particular logical reasoning process, called deduction.

Through deduction, one can derive specific statements from general ones. For example, the theory of classical mechanics implies that a heavy body exerts a force on other bodies. From this, it can be logically deduced that the earth exerts a force on the moon and vice versa. It cannot be logically deduced from this theory that all humans are mortal. The latter statement can instead be correctly deduced from a theory that describes how organisms decay and die over time. There are sound and unsound ways in which deduction can be done and it can happen that scientists make incorrect deductions, which will inevitably seriously flaw their research. In the case of alcohol and aggression, the scientist may deduce a specific prediction from the combination of a specific cognitive neuroscientific theory about how a particular brain process constitutes a person's emotional response with a biochemical theory about how alcohol has an impact on certain neurochemical processes in the brain. This novel combination of theories might lead him to offer a new detailed prediction regarding how alcohol use might lead to more aggressive responses. In the case of the interdisciplinary study of poverty, researchers had to consider whether their integrated insights into the socio-economic and psychological effects of poverty could be correctly deduced and were consistent with the existing theories on poverty. The process of deduction in humanities research is not always equally clear, as in physics or cognitive science, as phenomena in that domain tend to be determined by more than just a single set of factors. Nonetheless, when a humanities scholar aims to interpret a particular symbol or painting, she will still present a relevant knowledge base from which it might be deduced that the object under scrutiny can be interpreted in a specific way.

Often, one can find the term 'hypothesis' used interchangeably with 'prediction', yet the two are not identical. A hypothesis offers a specific explanation or insight into a phenomenon that can be put to the test and is based upon a scientist's expertise, rather than upon a specific set of data. Scientists then often proceed to compare a 'null hypothesis' – according to which the conjectured explanatory relation does not exist – with their 'alternative hypothesis'. Such educated guesses are indispensable in science, yet should be distinguished from predictions or conjectures that rely more specifically upon already existing data.

Operationalization and investigation of reality

The third component of the Science Cycle refers to the world or reality. Before a scientist can put his prediction to the test, she needs to think creatively about a reliable way to do this. It is one thing to deduce from the existing body of knowledge that there must be a connection between alcohol use and a person's responses; it is quite another and complex thing to develop an experiment and instrument to investigate this in a precise way. The scientist must think of how to operationalize her prediction and what investigation might be sufficient to study the operationalized prediction. Such an investigation may require experimentation, but it might also require different forms of study, such as archive research or in-depth interviews with subjects. That said, in order for other scientists to be able to check and control the findings of others, the operationalization must be such that it can be repeated and reproduced by others at other locations and times.

In the case of our example on the relation between alcohol and aggression, questions emerge such as: what are the relevant neurochemical compounds to be investigated? Are these compounds directly or indirectly affected by the influx of alcohol into the body? What brain areas are relevant and how can we find out whether these have any effects on a person's behavior? What instruments do we need to use to detect these effects, and what behavioral changes can we use as an indicator of aggression? Who might we use as guinea pigs for such experiments or observations, and what is the appropriate amount (ethically and health-wise) of alcohol that they should drink, in what period of time? What statistical methods can we use to analyze the data that our experiment might yield in order to determine whether its results are valid and significant? Comparable questions have to be answered by the humanities scholar or the social scientist who has developed a prediction or conjunction about, for example, the meaning of a particular symbol in the Renaissance, or the power relations that have influenced its meaning. The humanities scholar might want to operationalize her question by focusing on the use of such a symbol in paintings, which requires her to combine insights from plant iconology with those about Renaissance paintings to suggest a probable interpretation of the symbol at stake. The social scientist, in turn, might want to focus on a particular religious crisis and seek to understand this by employing a structuralist theory of power and combine it with insights about how, in that particular religion, social hierarchical relations are justified. In other words, humanities scholars and social scientists also need to determine how to relate general theories or previous insights into particular objects or events in order to understand the object of their investigation.

Data collection and observation and induction: Toward theories and laws

Having deduced from one or more theories a particular prediction or conjunction, and having operationalized these in such a way that a study or investigation of a particular object or event in the world is possible, the scientist will now be able to collect and observe certain results, data, or facts. Part of the collection and observation of facts also entails, of course, their analysis; for example, the statistical analysis of data on individuals' alcohol use combined with the data on their response changes. At this stage, sense perception is involved, but you will realize that this perception is facilitated in crucial ways by processes such as theorizing, reasoning, operationalization, and experimentation and by the use of specific methods and instruments (e.g. computer software to run your statistical tests), which have been developed over time via similar processes in previous decades or even centuries by fellow scientists. Indeed, philosophers of science often refer to this entanglement of observation with the other processes of the Science Cycle by referring to the 'theory-ladenness' of observations.

In short, the perception that scientists rely upon is, in many ways, very different from the perception that lay persons refer to when they mention their own observations as support for their statements. Lay persons sometimes believe that there are 'naked facts' that inevitably lead any sensible person to a particular conclusion. You will probably understand by now that even unscientific perceptions are dependent upon the knowledge and beliefs that someone has. Most adults will agree that the perception that the earth is flat is an illusion caused by the fact that it is nearly impossible to perceive, with the naked eye, the slight curvature of the earth – yet children might still insist on the earth being flat. Yet, even if a sensible lay person has reliably witnessed a series of events, she may still be mistaken in the conclusion that she draws from it. This brings us to the last process involved in the Science Cycle – induction.

As mentioned at the beginning, science builds upon sense perception, logically sound reasoning processes, and the accumulated results of previous generations of scientists. When we started to discuss the figure of the Science Cycle, we began with the most important component of science', that is to say, the theories, concepts, and insights that are characteristic of science. Yet, where do these theories, concepts, and insights come from, and how did they emerge? Surely, they must somehow be founded on facts or on data. It is difficult to give a straight answer to this question for two reasons. One reason is that by entering the Science Cycle, each scientist builds upon the work of her predecessors, which also implies – as we noted above – that all scientifically acquired facts and observations are 'theory-laden'. It is impossible to do science and to gather data without somehow relying upon previously developed theories, as these have contributed to the development of the instruments, procedures, analytical techniques, and other elements of data acquisition. So theories do not just emerge from data alone, but are being built – perhaps indirectly – on other theories as well.

And there is a second reason why theories and concepts are not merely derived from facts or data and it has to do with the problem of induction. Alongside deduction, induction is the most important logical reasoning process that scientists use in their work, but it is far more complicated than deduction. For example, there are many ways in which one can deduce multiple particular statements in a perfectly logical way from a general statement or theory: if all animals are mortal, for example, one can deduce that birds are mortal, and that mammals are mortal, and that Socrates is mortal, and so on. Making an inference in the other direction with induction, however, is never perfect or completely reliable. If, for example, one has found that birds reproduce sexually, and that mammals reproduce sexually, and that Socrates has reproduced sexually, it is still not correct to infer from this that all animals reproduce sexually. Indeed, further investigation would reveal that not only quite a few plants reproduce asexually, but also some insects, amphibians, and reptiles do so via unfertilized eggs. Unfortunately, inducing a generally valid theory from a limited set of facts or data is logically never completely warranted and therefore always tricky.

Indeed, any data set is inevitably limited as the future or past may, here or elsewhere in the universe, yield unexpected facts. The scientists in our example may, at some point, have found data to support their general theory that alcohol abuse tends to lead to increased aggression in humans, but it has been discovered more recently that persons with a particular genetic mutation are able to decompose alcohol much better than most people. Their induction has turned out to be flawed and they will have to adjust and specify their theory, making it less general, by accounting for the exception that scientists are now aware of.

Nonetheless, if we want to expand our knowledge we cannot do so without using induction at some point. Yet, it is important to realize the inevitable risk involved in induction and to develop counter-measures that help to mitigate that risk. We will deal with such a counter-measure shortly. Before doing so, it is appropriate to mention here the lesson that the previously quoted philosopher of science Karl Popper drew from this precarious nature of induction. He insisted that since induction is always precarious and we can never infer a true general statement with utter certainty from observed facts, scientists should give up proving a theory true and instead aim to disprove incorrect theories. In Popper's words: they should devote their efforts to 'falsification' instead of 'verification'. For such a falsification or proof of falseness we only need a single observation, as that single observation is sufficient to teach us the important lesson that our current theory is not yet adequate. Generally, scientists do not comply entirely with Popper's advice and tend to adopt both strategies, i.e. they check whether a particular theory might easily be falsified or disproved, but they also seek to confirm (another) theory by gathering further support for it.

Some final remarks: Pluralism and assumptions

Popper's critique of verification points to an important insight: merely repeating the same experiment or investigation over and over again might yield a huge collection of data yet still fail to prove a theory's truth. Conducting a more robust scientific investigation requires the use of a plurality of methods and theories. As mentioned above, given the complex and dynamic nature of many phenomena, a single theory is often not sufficient to understand these completely. For the relation between alcohol and aggression we have to combine genetic, social scientific, and psychological theories, for example. Similarly, our methods of investigation should be diverse. This means that if the connection between alcohol use and aggressive responses in our group of subjects is founded not just on investigations focusing on the psychological level, but also on the group level and on the genetic level, our inference – or induction – to a causal connection is more trustworthy than if it rested upon a single research method and its associated theories. Not surprisingly, interdisciplinary research by its very nature implies theoretical and methodological pluralism. This brings its own difficulties but usually also yields more robust results than monism does.

Finally, it is important to realize that although scientists need to be much more explicit and articulate about the theories and insights they use, and about the reasoning behind their predictions and conclusions, scientists still silently assume a lot when doing all this. Such assumptions are often based upon very specific expertise pertinent to a scientific field, but they can also have a much vaguer background. Implicit assumptions are associated with many features in science:

assumptions can pertain to the applicability of measuring instruments, to the number and nature of causes of a phenomenon, to the validity of a scientific conclusion to a domain of reality, and so on. For instance, most scientists nowadays silently assume that the universe will behave tomorrow according to the same laws as yesterday and today: if they did not believe this, their research would perhaps only be relevant for explaining today's phenomena. An assumption that has turned out to be false since the discovery of epigenetics is the assumption that DNA is the only carrier of inherited information across generations. More specifically, cognitive scientists have assumed for a long time that their main reliance upon Western psychology students as subjects would not have an impact upon the general validity of their studies of visual perception. This assumption has now been challenged, as it appears that socio-cultural differences do have an impact upon perception. Acceptation of this assumption could have far-reaching consequences for cognitive science and psychology, but there are understandable reservations against this.

Interdisciplinarians should particularly acknowledge scientific pluralism and the importance of assumptions. As interdisciplinary research consists of integrating insights from different sciences, notwithstanding their theoretical and methodological differences, understanding and recognizing the relevance of pluralism is a good starting point. Similarly, implicit assumptions can often prevent scientists from collaborating or learning from each other, while articulating these assumptions might facilitate this. The rejection of the assumption of DNA being the only carrier of inherited information with the discovery of epigenetic inheritance, for example, suggested that geneticists, ethologists, and developmental scientists could work together to explain the transmission of environmental stress or anxiety across generations, which, in turn, might be related to alcohol abuse. Similarly, recognizing that Western psychology students might not be representative of the global population in all respects has led to fruitful collaborations between cognitive scientists, cultural anthropologists, and sociologists.

With these remarks on pluralism and assumptions, we close this brief philosophical discussion on what science is. The ingredients that have been discussed in this chapter will return in what is to come below. But first we will discuss what disciplines are, since we are not doing 'science' in a general sense; rather, we are doing physics or cognitive science or history or European studies, and so on: science is organized in terms of disciplines.

4 Interdisciplinarity

Now that we know what academic disciplines are and how they emerged and developed, it is time to introduce interdisciplinarity. One of the most widely used and adequate definitions of interdisciplinarity comes from the National Academy of Sciences (2005):

> Interdisciplinary research is a mode of research in which an individual scientist or a team of scientists integrates information, data, techniques, tools, perspectives, concepts, and/or theories from two or more disciplines or bodies of specialized knowledge, with the objective to advance fundamental understanding or to solve problems whose solutions are beyond the scope of a single discipline or area of research practice.

Other definitions include those of Klein and Newell (1997), who define interdisciplinarity as "a process of answering a question, solving a problem, or addressing a topic that is too broad or complex to be dealt with adequately by a single discipline or profession [...] and draws on disciplinary perspectives and integrates their insights through construction of a more comprehensive perspective" (pp. 393-394). Interdisciplinarity has become a buzzword in scientific debates, and it has been identified by many research funding organizations in Europe and the United States as an important factor in future research. Although there is no single accepted definition of interdisciplinarity and the term is sometimes used interchangeably with multidisciplinarity and transdisciplinarity, it is important to distinguish and describe these three different manifestations of research.

The basic difference between these manifestations of research that spread beyond a discipline is the extent to which researchers aim for the integration or synthesis of (disciplinary) insights. Interdisciplinary research literally means research between disciplines, referring to the interaction of disciplines with each other. Indeed, the Social Science Research Council in New York, which first used the term 'interdisciplinary' around 1925, aimed to facilitate collaborations between the social scientific disciplines it did oversee (Klein, 1990). Such interaction may range from the mere communication and comparison of ideas, through the exchange of data, methods, and procedures, to the mutual integration of organizing concepts, theories, methodology, and epistemological principles. In multidisciplinary research, the subject under study is also approached from different angles, using different disciplinary perspectives. However, in that case neither the theoretical perspectives nor the findings of the various disciplines are integrated. Lastly, transdisciplinary research also involves actors from fields outside of the university, thereby allowing for the integration of academic and non-academic or experiential knowledge (Hirsch-Hadorn et al., 2008).

In this handbook, we will use the following definitions:
1   Multidisciplinary research is research that involves more than one discipline, but without integration. Results from the involved disciplines are compared and conclusions are subsequently drawn from each of the individual disciplines, but there is no integration of the disciplinary insights.
2   Interdisciplinary research is research in which relevant concepts, theories, and/or methodologies from different academic disciplines, as well as the results or insights these disciplines generate, are integrated.
3   Transdisciplinary research occurs when researchers collaborate with stakeholders from outside the academic world. Knowledge from outside the academic world, as well as stakeholder values, is integrated with academic knowledge. Together, these insights determine what problem is studied and how this is done, and which interventions are selected to address the problem.

Figure 6 illustrates these different approaches to research.

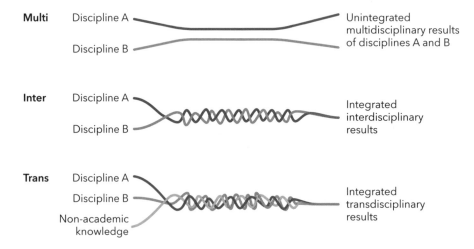

Figure 6   Multidisciplinarity, interdisciplinarity, and transdisciplinarity illustrated

Although in theory multi-, inter-, and transdisciplinarity can be distinguished, in practice researchers often switch between these approaches – sometimes within the same research project. For example, at the Dutch Research Institute for Transitions (DRIFT) researchers always go from trans- to inter- to multidisciplinarity (see the interview with DRIFT-director Dr. Derk Loorbach in chapter 13).
In the case of the alcohol and aggression research, scientists in a multidisciplinary team might shed light on the specific genetic and neurochemical and psychological

factors involved, often by conducting individually highly specialized disciplinary research. A further step then consists of the interdisciplinary integration of their insights by determining a specific genetic factor that modulates the neurochemical pathway along which alcohol affects an inhibitory process in subjects. This might then lead to a transdisciplinary research project involving alcoholics and their families, aimed at developing a socially robust intervention that prevents aggression.

7 The interdisciplinary research process

Although there are a lot of similarities between the disciplinary research process (with which you might already be familiar) and the interdisciplinary research process, there are some additional questions to answer, steps to perform, and challenges to overcome with regard toin the latter. We have therefore developed a model for doing interdisciplinary research (see box 5 and figure 9). Building on this model, we describe the different stages of the research process and the additional challenges interdisciplinary researchers are facing.

In part 1, we mentioned several drivers of interdisciplinary research, among which the inherent complexity of nature and society and the need to solve societal problems. However, in a student project you might not be pressured by such a driver to conduct interdisciplinary research, as the starting point may be different from academic research in practice. In some cases, students form a research team on the basis of their different educational backgrounds, and then collectively formulate a subject or a problem to investigate. Although the drivers described in part 1 might cover the problem or subject, the main driver in choosing a subject is usually the student's personal experience and practice.

7.1 The IIS model of interdisciplinary research

In figure 9 we present our model for interdisciplinary research. It describes a generalized research process, in which the following steps are distinguished: identify the problem or topic (i) and formulate the preliminary research question (ii) in the Orientation phase; develop the theoretical framework (iii), finalize the research question (iv) and sub-questions (vi) and research methods and design (vii) in the Preparation phase; collect and analyze the data (viii) in the Data phase; and interpret the results, draw conclusions and write the discussion (ix) in the Finalization phase. As convenient as this may seem, it is important to note that there is not really a standard research process, not only because research processes differ in practice, but also because what is considered a normal research process differs from discipline to discipline. Therefore, the model that is proposed here should serve as a guideline during your own research, not as a strict protocol.

In chapter 12, you will find an example of a complete interdisciplinary research project as carried out by students who used our model as a guideline. The example focuses on an innovative and sustainable form of greenhouse agriculture called Fogponics. It will help you to get an idea of how our research model can be operationalized.

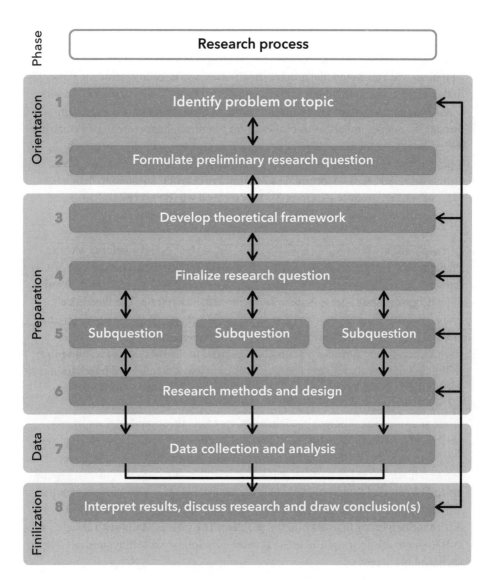

Phase

Research process

Orientation	1	Identify problem or topic
	2	Formulate preliminary research question
Preparation	3	Develop theoretical framework
	4	Finalize research question
	5	Subquestion / Subquestion / Subquestion
	6	Research methods and design
Data	7	Data collection and analysis
Finilization	8	Interpret results, discuss research and draw conclusion(s)

Figure 9   The IIS model for interdisciplinary research

In this model for the interdisciplinary research process, we use different steps (blue boxes in the middle of the figure) reflecting the tasks you must complete in a specific phase of your research (indicated in the left margin). Although you may sometimes need to return to a previous step, the order of steps is more or less fixed and you should not skip a single one. As an obvious example, you cannot analyze data that you have not yet collected. However, it is important to realize that you need to think one step ahead (i.e. you need to know how you are going to analyze your data before you start collecting them). For this reason, we have grouped together several steps in the following phases of the interdisciplinary research process: Orientation, Preparation, Data collection and analysis, and Finalization.

Phase 1   Orientation

You might start your research process by choosing a topic that fits your interests, or a problem that you would like to solve. In all cases, you need to explore the topic, find out which disciplines have something relevant to say about it, and then decide whether an interdisciplinary approach is justified at all. In short, you have to go through an orientation phase. A challenge for interdisciplinary research is ensuring each relevant discipline is reflected in the choice and wording of the research topic and that at this early point of the project no single discipline is dominant. Furthermore, you have to formulate a preliminary research question to define the focus of your research (see chapter 8). This forms the basis to create a theoretical framework (see chapter 9), which you will develop in the next phase.

Phase 2   Preparation

Preparing a scientific research requires the development of a theoretical framework, usually drawn from a literature search: scientists build upon the work of predecessors and colleagues, as was mentioned in chapter 2. The theoretical framework that must be developed is the result of a thorough literature research, gives an overview of the 'state of the art' (the most relevant theories and data on the research topic), and provides a systemized analysis of the most important findings. In the case of interdisciplinary research, this overview will consist of publications from different disciplines.

While analyzing the different disciplinary parts of the theoretical framework, you need to be constantly aware of the different disciplinary points of view (see figures 1 and 2 in chapter 1) with regard to the topic. This awareness of the differences between disciplinary perspectives will enable you to seek or create common ground (as will be explained in detail in chapter 10) at a later stage. As we have seen in part 1, finding common ground forms the basis for the integration of (some of) the different disciplinary insights into the problem. The integration of such insights will enable you to ask an insightful integrated interdisciplinary research question (step 4, explained in chapter 9).

After you have identified the common ground between the disciplines involved, it is time to think of the best way to answer your research question. What are the sub-questions arising from your main research question and which disciplines can address these questions? Please note that sub-questions can be both interdisciplinary and monodisciplinary.

In addition, you should also consider which methods and techniques are most suitable to answer the subquestions (see chapter 10). As mentioned in part 1, it is important to note that the chosen method(s) and technique(s) partly determine the kinds of results you will obtain. In certain cases, it will be useful to integrate multiple disciplinary research methods and techniques in order to get to a more complete answer to your questions (see chapter 10).

When you have (i) identified the problem; (ii) formulated a preliminary research question; (iii) developed an integrated theoretical framework; (iv) finalized the research question; and (v) designed a research outline (developed a methodology) to answer the research question, you will have completed the theoretical stage of your research. You should now have the information necessary to write a research proposal or literature study.

It may appear strange that conceiving a research proposal consumes so much time and attention. However, on second thought the reason for this should be obvious. As you can imagine, writing a research proposal is a crucial part of your research, as you need to formulate and plan the entire project before you begin collecting data. So, the more effort you put into writing a well-thought-out and integrated interdisciplinary research proposal, the more likely it is that your interdisciplinary research project will be a success.

Remember that by doing interdisciplinary research, you will be entering a field that is possibly completely new to you and perhaps even to your supervisor. As you will be connecting disciplines and fields, you will most likely be unable to rely on your prior disciplinary experience to guide you. You will therefore need to set out a detailed, clear-cut process to guide you as you try to engage in the holistic thinking required for interdisciplinary integration. The model for interdisciplinary research will serve as a general guideline, but you need to map out in detail how you will apply its guidelines to your specific project, and you have to do so in advance so that you will not flounder in the morass of (sometimes conflicting) disciplinary details in which you will soon find yourself (W.H. Newell, pers. comm., 3 December 2013). It is important to keep in mind that along the road you may discover several other disciplinary insights that somehow touch upon your problem. However, in the preparation phase you have investigated what the most relevant disciplinary contributions to answering your research question are and therefore you should not always feel tempted to include those later discoveries.

Phase 3   Data collection and analysis

After your research proposal has been completed and accepted, you can begin the practical stage of your research and start collecting data – of whatever nature they may be. This phase starts off with the operationalization of your main questions and sub-questions into research methods in order to obtain data. Once you have collected the data needed to answer your questions, you have to think about ways to analyze the data (see chapter 11).

Phase 4   Finalization

Although some research projects might invite an implementation of the results, we will here stick to the research process itself. As presenting research results always entails a consideration of its limitations and future extensions or follow-ups, we will finish the process by providing a discussion and conclusion. Formulating a discussion and conclusion in interdisciplinary research might be more difficult than in monodisciplinary research. You have to integrate the results and insights related to your sub-questions and you also have to ensure that you actually answer your research question and reflect on your answer by referring to your integrated theoretical framework. The differences and overlap you have found between different disciplinary insights in the theoretical stage of your research will help you to understand the implications of your results and will give more insight into the topic.

It is important to note that the research process is an iterative process, a process in which a cycle of operations is usually executed more than once, gradually bringing one closer to some optimal condition or goal. You will start with a topic or question and finish with a conclusion, but in between you will most probably need to go back and forth between the different phases of the research process. This 'movement' is likely to affect your research question, which you may need to rephrase during different stages of the research. Conversely, if you have made changes to your theoretical framework, your discussion and conclusion will not remain the same as these will refer to that framework. Especially in the preparation phase, iteration is likely to be important. As you collect more information, this will continuously influence your research question.

7.2 Planning your research project

As you can imagine, an interdisciplinary research project is a major assignment that requires even more planning than 'normal' research, especially when you are working in a team. A lot of time has to be invested in the coordination of the different subprojects and communication between the contributing researchers. More than in monodisciplinary research, interdisciplinary research demands openness and flexibility of the academic as well as collegiality when you are working as a team. As you can imagine, the different (disciplinary) sub-projects are likely to be executed at different moments of time, as – for example – the results of one sub-project might form the starting point of a second sub-project. Therefore, it is highly important to think about a sound planning when you are about to begin an interdisciplinary research project. Of course, some parts of the project can turn out to be more time consuming than expected. It is particularly important to realize that composing and writing your final research report can take a considerable amount of time. Thus, try to make a flexible planning to be able to cope with such unexpected surprises, and try to leave some time at the end of the project open to be able to finish the final report in a good way. The time schedule for a six-month bachelor-level research project is likely to resemble the one displayed in figure 10.

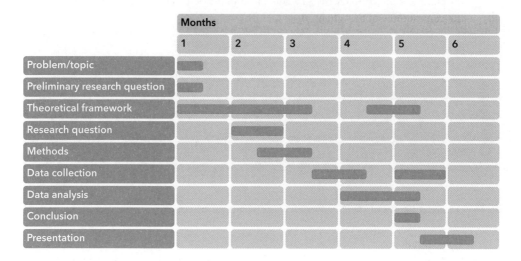

Figure 10   Time schedule for a bachelor research project

8 The problem

After the first preview of the IIS model of interdisciplinary research, we will now zoom in on the different phases and guide you through the steps of the model in more detail. In any research project, the first task at hand is to narrow down the problem or topic to a research question that can be answered in the time available. Especially in interdisciplinary research this can be a challenging step as it always involves a complex problem (see chapter 5), which can (and should be) be studied from multiple perspectives or disciplines. Here, we will describe the first two steps of our interdisciplinary research model (figure 11). How to narrow down a complex problem to a preliminary research question that is feasible in both time and scale is the central topic of this chapter.

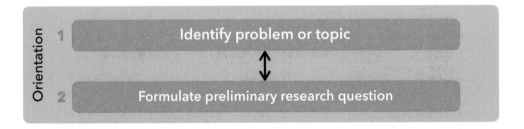

Figure 11   Steps 1 and 2 of the IIS model for interdisciplinary research

Considerations:
- Consider all relevant disciplines: which 3 to 4 disciplines are most relevant?
- What are the dominant perspectives of those disciplines on the problem or area of interest?

Step 1   Identify problem or topic

Finding a topic is not always easy. An additional challenge in the case of student projects is to find a problem that can be addressed by the available disciplinary expertise in the research team (see box 5 for an exercise that you can use when trying to find a shared topic of interest). But it is equally important to find something that triggers your academic curiosity.

Box 5

Brainstorm exercise: Finding a shared topic of interest via 'triangulation'

If an interdisciplinary team consists of a given combination of disciplines it may be somewhat challenging to develop a shared topic as usually scientists start with a topic and then assemble the necessary team. However, determining the 'overlap' between several disciplines can be done by performing a 'triangulation' exercise. The term triangulation refers to the process that, for example, allows mobile phone providers to precisely determine the position of your mobile phone at the intersection of three or more antennas' areas.

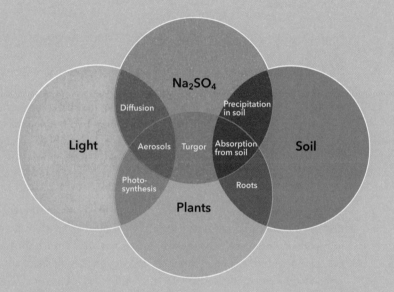

An example of triangulation: combining insights from chemistry, geography, plant physiology and physics, a group of students has decided to investigate the impact of sodium sulphate from volcanic eruptions on the environment and particularly in plants (Gelauff, Gravemaker, Isarin & Waajen, 2015).

You might similarly determine a specific and shared topic by together following these steps:

▼

1   Write down individually and from your disciplinary perspective a list of topics that interest you, taking into account what might be of interest to other disciplines.
2   Exchange the different lists of topics with each other and look for one or more topics that show similarity or overlap with others.
3   Consider individually what sub-questions arising from such topics your discipline could answer and formulate a preliminary research question.
4   Again, discuss in the team the different topics and the sets of sub-questions related to those topics that each member has formulated, choosing the most relevant or fruitful topic for further elaboration.

Sometimes a brainstorm session can lead to the discovery of a knowledge gap that can be addressed with an interdisciplinary research question. A student who was educated in both law and interdisciplinary social sciences found an interesting discrepancy between the two fields. In literature from the fields of political science and sociology, he found explanations for the fact that in the Netherlands in recent years there had been an increase in the societal call for stricter penalties for criminal acts. Theories from the field of law, on the other hand, provided convincing arguments against strong punishments.

The question why the societal call for stricter penalties continues to exist, despite the strong arguments from judges that stronger punishment does not work had not yet been asked, and thus not answered. It provided the basis for an interdisciplinary research project on the effects of societal and political criticism on the judiciary in the Netherlands (Noyon, 2012).

Once you have decided on a topic or a problem that you want to focus on in your project, you need to set a starting point for your research. The answers to the following questions can be a good starting point for your initial literature research, and they can help to clarify the context of your topic of research.
1   What do I already know about the problem?
2   What aspects, related to the problem, are important to consider?
3   What other problems does it relate to?
4   From which perspectives can I look at this problem?

It can be very helpful to visualize your answers to these questions in a concept map or a similar illustration. For example, the mind map below (figure 12) was built around the topic of disaster risk reduction. Drawing a mind map in which you visualize as many relevant aspects pertaining to the topic as possible can help you to decide on a preliminary research question (Step 2 of the research model).

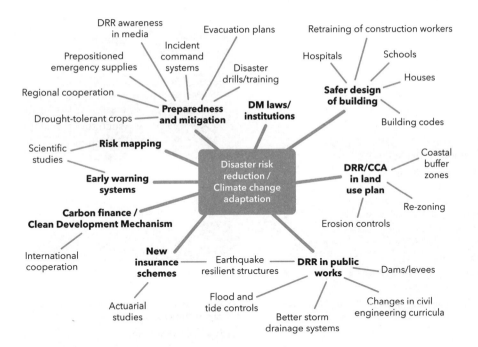

Figure 12 Example of a mind map (Talisayon, 2010). Reprinted with permission from the author

Another way to reveal the most relevant aspects pertaining to the research topic is the development of a mechanistic model, which is commonly used in the life sciences and the cognitive sciences and is gradually being adopted in the social sciences as well. Discussing it here may also help you to realize how the different steps in the interdisciplinary research process are connected with each other, because a mechanistic model can be useful both when you are developing your research question and when attempting to integrate new results from your interdisciplinary research. Take, for example, the mechanistic or mechanism-based explanation of action understanding, which helps to explain how humans are capable of understanding other people's actions at several levels of complexity. Interdisciplinary research by cognitive neuroscientists, hermeneutic scholars, and others can clarify the complex cognitive mechanisms that develop over time, enabling humans to understand actions that consist not just of bodily behavior but of verbally expressed intentions and narratives as well (Keestra, 2012). Let us pause for a moment to see how this works and how such an approach can be useful at several phases of the interdisciplinary research process.

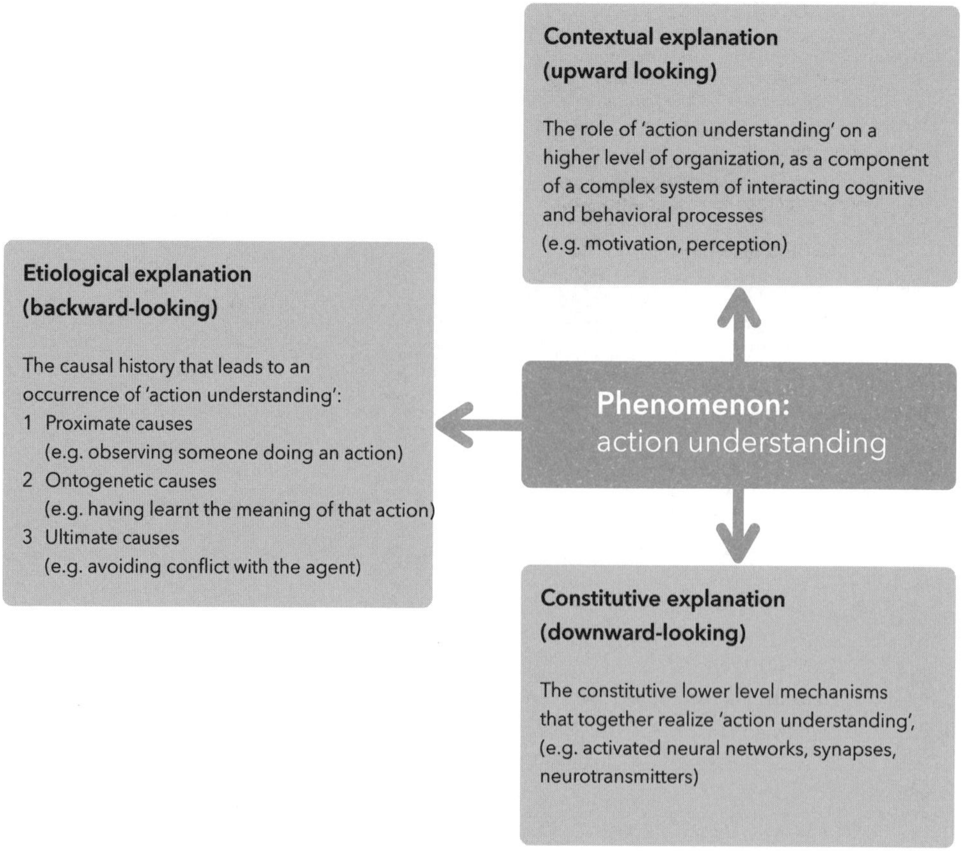

**Contextual explanation
(upward looking)**

The role of 'action understanding' on a
higher level of organization, as a component
of a complex system of interacting cognitive
and behavioral processes
(e.g. motivation, perception)

**Etiological explanation
(backward-looking)**

The causal history that leads to an
occurrence of 'action understanding':
1 Proximate causes
   (e.g. observing someone doing an action)
2 Ontogenetic causes
   (e.g. having learnt the meaning of that action)
3 Ultimate causes
   (e.g. avoiding conflict with the agent)

Phenomenon:
action understanding

**Constitutive explanation
(downward-looking)**

The constitutive lower level mechanisms
that together realize 'action understanding',
(e.g. activated neural networks, synapses,
neurotransmitters)

*Figure 13   Different explanations of a phenomenon, for example the phenomenon 'action
understanding' by a human subject (adapted from Valli, 2011)*

Figure 13 shows how scientists can develop and integrate different types of
explanation in order to reach a more comprehensive explanation of a particular
phenomenon, like a case of action understanding, or the decrease of fish stocks
in the North Sea, or the financial crisis in the EU. The figure suggests that we can
approach such a phenomenon from various perspectives that together might offer a
more comprehensive explanation. Obviously, a complex phenomenon is constituted
by component mechanisms, such as when many activated neural networks together
constitute action understanding, or when the financial situation is determined
by markets, institutions, selling and buying behaviors, and so on. Similarly, the
phenomenon (as much as its component mechanisms, like the ones just mentioned)
can be partly explained by looking into its history, in which both short- and
long-term processes play distinctive roles. In addition, one could also consider
how the phenomenon itself responds to its context: the phenomenon of action
understanding is also interacting with other cognitive and behavioral processes, fish
stock is responsive to a wider eco-system and the EU participates in global financial
networks.

What may become apparent to you from looking at figure 13 is that when you are collaborating with scientists from different perspectives you might still contribute to explaining the same phenomenon. Yet it also suggests that it takes an additional effort to ensure that your investigations are coordinated with each other; otherwise it can happen, for example, that the etiological explanation offered by a developmental scientist might be only indirectly related to the genetic explanation developed by a colleague and not even touch upon the sociological explanation suggested by yet another colleague. It would be better if you search for a research topic that facilitates such coordinated research together, such as when the cognitive process investigated by the developmental scientist is probably determined by genes that are available for genetic screening and is also involved in a form of social interaction. Discussing a phenomenon's comprehensive explanation, possibly with the help of a visual representation, might be helpful in this process.

The result of such collaborations is that the insights into a phenomenon – in the form of mechanistic explanation or otherwise – will, over time become more and more elaborated. A good example of an increasingly detailed and specified mechanistic explanation is the climate model that is developed by the IPCC (Le Treut, Somerville, Cubasch, Ding, Mauritzen et al., 2007). Through the years, climate scientists discovered additional components that are part of the mechanism that constitute our climate system. The evolution of the model of the explanatory mechanism from the 1970s onwards is illustrated in Figure 14.

This again suggests how such a model can be useful at various stages of research. Obviously, a mechanistic model is valuable as it can be employed as an integration technique for your results and theory (for other practical tips on how to come to an integrated research question, see chapter 10). However, in the context of identifying a problem or topic, a closer look at such a model might also be fruitful. For example, by scrutinizing the models, one might develop predictions or hypotheses about the involvement of oceans not only in absorbing sulphates and other substances, but also in absorbing and reflecting sunlight radiation. Indeed, it can be very useful for an interdisciplinary team to start its research by discussing one or more of such models.

The World in Global Climate Models

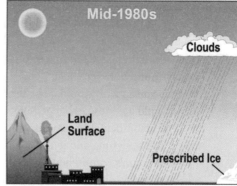
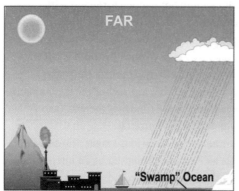
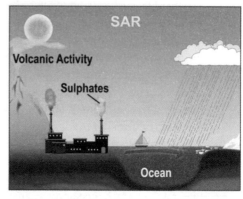
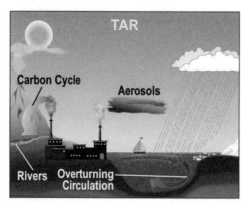
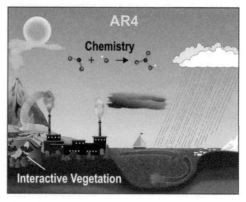

Figure 14   The evolution of climate change models as developed by the IPCC (Le Treut, Somerville, Cubasch., Ding, Mauritzen et al., 2007). Reprinted with permission from the author.

Once you have identified the problem or topic, you need to know from which perspectives the problem can be addressed. A first important consideration here is to identify the disciplines that are most relevant to the problem or topic. When you consider all relevant theories and methods, which 3 or 4 disciplines are most important for researching the problem? Subsequently, you can flesh out these perspectives: what are those disciplines' dominant perspectives on the problem or area of interest?

How do you select the most important disciplines for your problem? A good starting point would be the overview of disciplines and their main topics put together by Szostak [and presented in Repko (2012)]. Another way is to go through the content pages and introduction of introductory textbooks, pertinent encyclopedias, and compendiums that cover a field, relevant conference proceedings, or other comprehensive volumes. Such carefully edited volumes offer overviews that are very hard to get from browsing on the internet or in digital libraries. While going through the content pages and the introduction, you will usually be able to identify the phenomena studied, the main assumptions, and the more general theories of the field. This can provide a good starting point from which to gain an understanding of the different perspectives and assumptions that different fields take for granted (and thus no longer question). However, bear in mind that these textbooks are written by authors who are not necessarily self-reflective about the fundamental assumptions of their field (W.H. Newell, pers. comm., 3 December 2013). As a result, you may need at a certain point to articulate those assumptions and articulate other specific elements of a discipline in order to integrate its insights with those from other disciplines.

Other particularly helpful sources of information at the start of your literature research are review articles. In a review article, a researcher (or group of researchers) answers a research question or maps the state-of-the-art knowledge regarding a theme or a problem by analyzing and integrating the results of tens or sometimes even hundreds of relevant research articles. These review articles are a good source for getting an up-to-date overview of the perspectives within a field on a subject or problem.

With the knowledge you have now gained, you can refine your concept map into a more theoretically informed concept map. For example, take a look at figure 15, which presents a concept map concerning the subject of major depressive disorder.

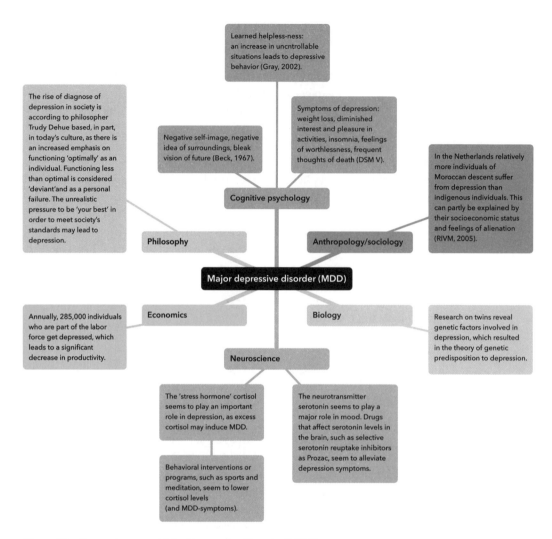

Figure 15   Concept map on Major Depressive Disorder (MDD)

Step 2   Formulate preliminary research question

At this point, you have decided on a topic, identified disciplines relevant to that topic, and created a concept map in which the main disciplinary theoretical perspectives are presented. This concept map will help you to formulate a preliminary research question. It is a preliminary research question because you will refine and adjust it according to the theoretical and methodological insights that you will gather when developing a theoretical framework (the next step in the research process; see figure 9). However, you do need a preliminary research question, as this will guide you to finding relevant theories and research in your fields of interest. Without a clear focus – a specific research question, in this case - on what you want to research within your topic of choice, it is easy to get lost in the vast amount of academic literature. When setting up a preliminary research question, try to avoid specific disciplinary biases as they may complicate interdisciplinary collaboration and integration further down the road. If possible, at this early stage, avoid unnecessary jargon, technical terms, or even non-technical terms that are characteristically used by academics from one discipline. One way to avoid these disciplinary terms is to try to formulate the problem in everyday language. Do not get discouraged when the terms are vague or imprecise, because this may be an advantage, insofar as it admits multiple interpretations that may offer as many clues to different disciplines. Some researchers find it troublesome, for example, that there are many different definitions of consciousness, whereas others contend that, as a result, many different research approaches to consciousness are invited, which eventually might come together in a more complete explanation of this complex phenomenon. In other words, during subsequent steps of the interdisciplinary process, you will probably re-examine the definition of the problem, and develop more precise wording that is responsive to all the relevant perspectives (Newell, 2007).

Examples of research questions that are not reasonably narrowed down:

- How can we improve sustainable agriculture?
- Is the judiciary affected by criticism?
- What is the best cure for depression?

Problems with the previous research questions are, amongst others, that results from previous research, which are usually much more specific, have not been incorporated in the question (i.e. 'How can we improve sustainable agriculture?'), contain concepts that lack specificity (i.e. 'judiciary' and 'criticism') or ask for too many possible conditions to investigate (i.e. 'What is the best cure for depression?'). Examples of research questions that are reasonably narrowed down:

- To what extent can fogponics contribute to sustainable agriculture?
- What are the effects of societal and political criticism on the judiciary in the Netherlands?
- To what extent can the medication selective serotonine reuptake inhibitors (SSRIs) increase the effectiveness of cognitive behavioral therapy in patients diagnosed with depression?

Your ultimate research question has to meet more criteria. Although you will check later on, when you finalize your research question, whether your research question is relevant, anchored, researchable, and precise, it can help to have these criteria in the forefront of your mind when you work on your preliminary research question (see also figure 16). The goal is a finalized research question that is:

Relevant: It should be related to the broader problem you wish to address, reflect the reason for your research project, and be the driver for interdisciplinary research. In short, it should be clear why it is worthwhile to seek an answer to the question.

Anchored: It should be the logical outcome of your literature review, expert interviews, and theoretical framework. Your research question has to be embedded in the fields of knowledge of your research topic, and the result should be of added value to the fields involved.

Researchable: It should be possible to conceive research methods that can address the question in the amount of time and with the means available.

Precise: It should be straightforward and specific. It should be clear what the research focus is.

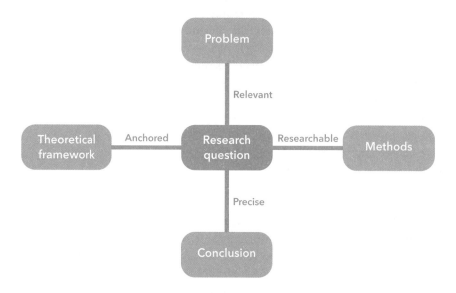

Figure 16   Defining characteristics of the research question: Relevant to the broader problem that is to be addressed, anchored in the theoretical framework, researchable with the methods at hand, and leading to a precise and straightforward conclusion

One more thing to keep in mind when developing a research question is that your finalized research question should incorporate all relevant perspectives. Try to avoid a one-sided question, for example by leaning too much to one discipline's theory. At the same time, you have to make sure that the question is not too general in nature and relates to a specific element of the topic.

9 Theoretical framework and research question[1]

It is now time to turn the preliminary research question into a researchable research question. By developing a theoretical framework that addresses your preliminary research question, you will be able to describe the 'state of the art' in your field of interest, sharpen your ideas, and then formulate a better, more specified research question. This part of the research process is described in this paragraph (and displayed in figure 17).

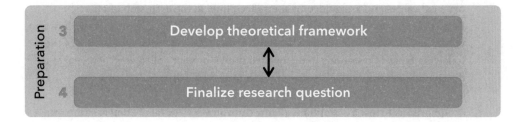

Figure 17   Steps 3 and 4 of the IIS Model for interdisciplinary research

Considerations:
- Consider all relevant theories, concepts, and assumptions that each discipline can contribute.
- Where do disciplinary theories overlap? Where can you find or create common ground?
- Is it possible to integrate the theoretical frameworks of the relevant disciplines?

As discussed in chapter 6, communication between (disciplinary) perspectives is a first important step towards integrating these perspectives. So an important question is how to enhance communication within your interdisciplinary research group? First and foremost, an understanding of one's own discipline is needed if a useful conversation between academics from different disciplines is to occur. In other words, one should be familiar with the theories, concepts, and methodologies that are central to one's discipline and realize how these and other ingredients make up

---

1   The authors thank Coyan Tromp for allowing them to make use of her work on data management tables in this chapter.

the Science Cycle according to which scientific research of your topic is conducted (see chapter 2 on what science is). One could also answer the following questions as a way of bringing the disciplinary perspective to the forefront (partly after Paul & Elder, 2014):

- What is your disciplinary perspective on the problem?
- Which insights is this perspective based on?
- What are the strengths and weaknesses of this perspective?
- What are the borders of your disciplinary perspective in researching the problem? That is to say: where do you see opportunities to collaborate with other disciplines?

The second and arguably the most important skill to enhance communication (and thus integration) across disciplines is critical self-reflection. Different methodologies to enhance conversation between academics of different disciplines have emerged, and they all stress the importance of academics' self-reflection on their (disciplinary) assumptions, mindset, and background. Lélé and Norgaard (2005), for example, emphasize that all researchers operate with implicit assumptions that are based on personal values and are guided by their discipline, to the exclusion of others. Reflecting on your personal values and assumptions can be a daunting task: how can you reflect on ideas you may not hold on a conscious level? You could think of the following types of questions to uncover your own or your colleagues' personal and disciplinary assumptions (based on the Socratic method):

- Questions aimed at clarification ('Can you explain...?')
- Questions to test assumptions ('How can you verify or falsify that assumption?')
- Questions that determine the argumentation ('Can there be a reason to question this evidence?')
- Questions to explore alternative perspectives ('Can someone else have a different perspective on this?')
- Questions that determine implications and consequences ('What would happen if...?')
- Questions that question the question ('What is the goal of this question?')

Thirdly, as explained in chapter 6, a main precondition for interdisciplinary integration is the ability of researchers to explain their different backgrounds, perspectives, and insights into the research problem. Practically, this means one has to be able to articulate and communicate one's perspective in a way that someone who does not share this specific disciplinary background can comprehend. For example, when explaining one's perspective, avoid using jargon or technical terms. It also means, when a colleague from another discipline is explaining her perspective, one has to dare to ask (critical) questions. Critical, open, and respectful communication with academics from other disciplines is one way to discover the assumptions underlying a discipline. This may be harder for solo interdisciplinarians, who may uncover disciplinary assumptions by observing cognitive dissonance, parsing a problem into components, critical thinking, and other modes of intellectual problem solving (W.H. Newell, pers. comm., 3 December 2013).

When engaging in communication with someone from another field, it can be useful to consider the following questions regarding the way someone else is communicating her perspective (after Paul & Elder, 2014):

- Does the researcher clarify key concepts when necessary? Are the concepts used justifiably?
- Does the researcher show sensitivity to what she is taking for granted or assuming?
- Does the researcher use questionable assumptions without addressing problems which might be inherent in those assumptions?
- Does the researcher show sensitivity to alternative relevant points of view or lines of reasoning? Does she consider and respond to objections framed from other relevant points of view?

Step 3   Develop theoretical framework

With the preliminary research question in mind, you have to do literature research in order to develop a theoretical framework. Such a framework can be defined as a comprehensive explanation of some aspect of the natural or social world that is supported by a vast body of evidence, generating testable and falsifiable predictions. This theoretical framework can serve as the 'backbone' of your research question and will help you to select the information or knowledge that is most relevant for your research. In addition, it can help you identify the most useful methods for studying this topic.

Note that the development of a theoretical framework is an ongoing process: you will be working on the framework throughout (the first half of) your research project. As your research progresses and you learn more about the research topic, you will also need to update your theoretical framework. This means that you have to constantly switch (or iterate) between your research question (and sub-questions), your theoretical framework, and your methods. Your integrated theoretical framework will ultimately be a substantial part of your research proposal and final report. In addition, by constructing it early in the research process, it can also serve as a tool for developing a relevant and firmly anchored research question. The following tasks are important in creating a theoretical framework:

- Collecting disciplinary insights into the problem.
- Analyzing the nature of differences between these insights.
- Finding or creating common ground through the use of different integration techniques.

Below we explain in more detail what these tasks entail.

1   Collecting disciplinary insights into the problem

It is important to have an overview of the research in your field of interest. To gain insight into the 'state of the art' of the relevant disciplines, you will need to find out which ideas and theories have already been developed through research within these different disciplines. Academic disciplines organize and store their knowledge by means of specific journals and databases. So make sure you list the major journals and publications within the fields that are relevant to your research project. Another good starting point is an interview with an expert on the topic. An expert can help you to refine your literature search and choose the most relevant perspectives to research a topic.

In order to begin constructing an integrated theoretical framework, you may need to create several more specific theoretical frameworks from different disciplines before you are able to decide on how to integrate their most relevant parts. The integrated theoretical framework should:

- offer a critical overview of relevant academic literature on your research topic and question;
- be based on perspectives and theories from each of the selected disciplines, preferably from more than one field (or sub-discipline) within each discipline;
- be a coherent story, as opposed to just a collection of concepts or theories, and show the reasoning behind the integrated perspectives that led to your research question.

For example, in the research project on fogponics (chapter 12) several theoretical frameworks pertaining to different disciplines had to be integrated in order to be able to address the research question: To what extent can fogponics contribute to sustainable agriculture? First, the students defined sustainable development as encompassing both environmental and economic stakes or needs, and they chose to focus on tomato plants and their nutrient and water use (based on insights from economics that tomatoes are an important export product for the Netherlands). Biologists had developed fogponics systems (where 'hanging' roots are provided with water in the form of fog), whereas chemists had developed a system that could help by measuring the use of nutrients (the so-called HPLC technique). Using additional theoretical frameworks from mathematics and artificial intelligence, the students could respectively simulate plant growth (to make comparisons to current greenhouse culture) and make the fogponics system as efficient as possible.

A useful tool for comparing disciplinary insights and understanding their basis is a data management table (after Repko, 2008; see figure 18), which lists the assumptions, theories, and methods of research from the relevant disciplinary literature on the subject. A data management table not only provides an overview of the relevant disciplinary insights into the research problem, later on in the research project it can also provide a basis for interdisciplinary integration at both the theoretical and the methodological level. Moreover, it provides an extremely useful tool for a team of researchers to assemble the ingredients that individual team members will be collecting.

Full reference to the book or article				
Discipline / sub-discipline	Theory / hypothesis	Concept(s)	Assumptions / methodology	Insight into problem
Name the specific research field and specialization.	Explain what it entails; describe the relation between the (f) actors that are considered or conjectured to be relevant (e.g. cause X and effects Y + Z, or the correlation between different (f)actors; or why a certain intervention is thought to be useful in helping to overcome the problem).	Analyze the key building blocks of the explanation or conceptualization captured in the theoretical framework. Give clear definitions of them. Explain which of the (potentially plural) definitions you will take as a point of departure in your research project.	Analyze the basic assumptions underlying your theoretical framework. Those assumptions can have an ontological, epistemological, methodological, or cultural philosophical nature, i.e. they can be related to our views on reality, and to our views on how we can gain knowledge about that reality, how we can best study that reality, and about how science can contribute to society. Explain which assumptions you will incorporate, or which you reject.	Explain how the theory and the key concepts it entails help to provide more insight in or a possible solution to the problem you are addressing. Take also into consideration possible limitations.

Figure 18 Data management table

How can you find the relevant research fields, theories, concepts, and assumptions for your interdisciplinary research? Below we provide a list indicating where you may find the various elements of the data management table.

Discipline / sub-discipline

To find out which discipline the insights you find useful for your research are coming from, the following questions may help:

- Check the title of the journal; what kind of research field is represented in the title?
- Check the affiliation of author(s). What kind of institution(s) or organization(s) are they working for? If you are not sure, look further on the internet to find more information about the author(s).
- Similarly, check the reference list attached to the article for prominent journal and book titles and other indications of their disciplinary backgrounds.
- Check the mind map you made when working on your preliminary research

question. What research fields are linked to your problem?

Theory

Finding out which theory lies at the basis of the insights you find useful can be hard. Here, we provide some advice on how to uncover it:

- Sometimes a prominent theory or hypothesis is explicitly named in an article, like the theory of evolution, the Marxist theory, or the Goldbach conjecture. It might even be taken up in the abstract. Then, it is only a matter of looking for a good description of what the theory states or, if you cannot find one in the article or book, to try and formulate it yourself.
  (Note: theories can be closely related to concepts. For tips on how to identify key concepts, see below.)
- When the theory is not explicitly stated in the article, it can usually be found in review articles. These types of articles not only provide the state-of-the-art theories in the research field, they often present and compare a variety of possible explanations. These alternative explanations may be similar, analogous explanations, but they may also be completely different and thus form a competitor for the theory favored by the particular research group whose article or book you are reading.
- Another strategy for finding out about what theory the author(s) adhere to is to try and find online information about the author(s) (see the suggestion above under 'discipline-sub-discipline').
- It may be helpful to make a theory map in which you summarize all the answers you have found about what exactly the theory entails, how it came into being, who coined the name, what contribution the theory can make to the field under study and, specifically, to your research topic, whether any data were found to support the theory, and what alternative and competitive interpretations exist.

Concepts

To identify the concepts that are relevant to your research project, the following guidelines are useful:

- Concepts answer the 'what' question: what is the research project about, i.e. what are the phenomena under investigation? To find the concepts, think of keywords that are also often listed on the first page of journal articles.
- Concepts often contain special, unusual terms and jargon. This is not always the case though; sometimes a common word is used in a particular way. That is why giving a clear definition of a concept is very important.
- The 'same' concept can often be found in different theories and different researchers might use them in the context of different theoretical frameworks, and may thus give different interpretations of such a concept. This holds for rationality, chaos and equilibrium, for example.
- Concepts can sometimes be difficult to distinguish from theories, principles, causal links, phenomena, or methods. It might help you to realize that a theory is an overarching framework and a concept is one of the defining key elements within that theory. But when the concept of, for instance, resilience is considered to be such a key driver that researchers start talking about resilience theory, the

distinction obviously becomes a bit blurred.

- 'Concept' is sometimes even used in a still broader sense, in the sense of approach or discourse.
- Just as with theories, it can be helpful to create a concept map in which you summarize all the answers you have found about what the concept exactly is, how it came into being, who coined the name, what contribution the concept can make to the theories in the field and, specifically, with regard to your research topic, whether any data were found to support the meaning and role of the concept, and what alternative and competitive interpretations exist of one and the 'same' concept.

Assumptions

The assumptions underlying a discipline are often implicit as scientists within a field share them without questioning these assumptions. Making these assumptions explicit can help to articulate differences or conflicts between disciplines – and scientists – and sometimes even to remove them. There are various kinds of assumptions:

- Ontological assumptions, concerning what is considered real and what not. Disciplines differ with respect to what they consider the building blocks (constituents) or reality and what they consider to be mere appearances. The ontological status of mathematical objects can be disputed, or of survival value, or of antimatter, or of consciousness, to give a few examples.
- Epistemological assumptions concern the question what can be known, and what not. Knowledge can be considered a valid 'mirror of reality', whereas others might think of knowledge as a mere instrument that works, or not, with yet others remaining quite skeptical about the nature and value of knowledge in general.
- Anthropological assumptions pertain to what it is to be human and about human needs, fears, values and the like. Such assumptions might be relevant for how scientists think about humans as their object of knowledge but also about their own position as scientists.
- Cultural and social assumptions often matter as well, as science is both a product of culture and society and produces results with an impact on these. Depending on how disciplines or scientists conceive of culture and society, they may reflect differently upon what science is and how it should function. The concept of the 'knowledge society' is based upon the assumption that knowledge and knowledge production is fundamental to our current society – which can be debated.
- Ethical assumptions are relevant when it comes to deciding about what scientific questions merits attention and money, choosing how to conduct a research project and especially about the implementation of scientific results. The use of science and scientific results by the military and in irresponsible environmental and social projects has led to questions about 'dual use' of these results and about the ethical neutrality of science and scientists.
- Methodological assumptions refer to implicit ideas about research strategies, methods for experimentation and analysis, and the like. Scientists can silently

assume that their colleagues share their ideas about valid and objective methods, even though all scientific methods have their limitations in terms of validity, objectivity, feasibility, and so on. Inter- and transdisciplinary research almost always uses a methodological pluralism, which requires scientists to articulate and reconsider these assumptions.

These kinds of assumptions are among the most relevant in the context of science. Note that we do not argue against having such assumptions: It is not wrong to implicitly assume that nature's laws will be the same tomorrow as they are today, for example, as it would be useless to do research if a scientist thought otherwise. Articulating and doubting this assumption about the behavior of the laws of nature is usually unnecessary. However, as Einstein's critique of Newton's law of gravity has shown, even a natural law might turn out to be conditional in ways that were previously unthinkable. In other words, the ontological assumption about material reality being unconditionally determined by a particular law-like relation turned out to be in need of revision. Similarly, the physicists assuming that the knowledge concerning this law was complete had to recognize the incorrectness of their assumption. Given its central role in Newtonian physics, the reconsideration and partial rejection of this assumption was a difficult process. Similar processes have taken place in other disciplines as well. Other examples are Darwin's rejection of the assumed purposeful nature of the evolution of natural kinds, or the rejection by behavioral economists of the assumption that economic decisions are always rational and not influenced by emotions.

It is good to realize that the critique of 'normal science' – in Kuhn's terms (see chapter 3) – often targets such assumptions and that scientific breakthroughs often consist of the rejection of an assumption that is implicitly accepted by a scientific community. Not all interdisciplinary or transdisciplinary research projects are revolutionary in this sense, obviously, yet they still require the articulation, discussion, and reconsideration of relevant assumptions by the team members. It is very helpful to use a data management table when doing so as you are required to articulate such assumptions that implicitly structure the disciplinary research being integrated in the project.

Below is an example of a data management table filled in with information on disciplinary research on the link between alcohol consumption and aggressive behavior.

Caetano, R., Schafer, J. & Cunradi, C.B. (2001). Alcohol-related intimate partner violence among White, Black, and Hispanic couples in the United States. Alcohol Research and Health, 25, 58-65

Discipline / sub-discipline	Theory / hypothesis	Concept(s)	Assumptions / methodology	Insight into problem
Psychology: Understanding behavior and mental processes of individuals by researching both groups of people and specific cases	**Subculture of violence theory:** Certain groups in society accept violence as a means of conflict resolution more than other groups	**Intimate Partner Violence (IPV):** Male-to-female/female-to-male intimate partner violence	**Higher rate found among female-to-male IPV:** May be due to underreporting of violence data across gender or because in clinical samples men are more violent	**Support for the subculture of violence theory:** Black subjects reported significantly higher female-to-male IPV (not male-to female IPV) than White subjects when controlled for factors such as socioeconomic background, drinking, and history of victimization
	Social structure theory: Socioeconomic factors that characterize the lives of specific groups	**Violence:** 11 (physical) violence items from the Conflict Tactics Scale: throwing, pushing, grabbing, shoving, slapping, kicking, biting, hitting, beating-up, choking, burning, forcing sex, threatening with knife or gun, stabbing, and/or shooting	**Coding alcohol consumption:** More than three drinks a day considered heavy drinking	The presence of drinking in an IPV incident does not mean that alcohol is the cause of the violence; it may also be explained by the **expectation that alcohol will disinhibit**, or that some people use alcohol as an excuse
Epidemiology: The study of patterns of health and illness and associated factors at the population level, identifying risk factors (for disease) and determining optimal treatment approaches to clinical practice and for preventive measures	**Acute effects hypothesis:** Alcohol disinhibits aggressive behavior	**Alcohol problem measures:** Survey with 29 alcohol-related problems from 14 specific problem areas	**Sample is representative** and can be applied to all couples in US but not to couples with alcohol-related problems that are uncommon	Individual level factors, characteristics of the relationship, and characteristics of the environment (social structure) form a constellation of factors resulting in IPV
	Alcohol as excuse hypothesis Alcohol is a convenient factor to excuse behavior that would otherwise be unacceptable		**The sample is limited:** Mostly 'moderate' violence in household sample, and showing only associations, not causations	
	Chronic effects hypothesis: People with a history of heavy drinking are predisposed to violence or drinking heavily (which leads to violence) due to other factors or have alcohol-exacerbated brain damage associated with violent outbursts	**Problem syndrome:** Clustering of problems in one area (e.g., alcohol dependence) with other factors (e.g., IPV); socio-demographic factors and psychosocial variables	**Coding ethnicity:** Black Hispanic, White Hispanic, Black not Hispanic, White not Hispanic (no mixed category)	Alcohol problems not always cause of IPV, but can be used as **marker for identifying population at (more) risk of IPV**
			Violence: Unreported violence does not count. Only reported physical violence not emotional abuse	

Figure 19 Example of a data management table

Fish, E.W, Faccidomo, S. & Miczek, K.A. (1999). Aggression heightened by alcohol or social instigation in mice: Reduction by the 5-HT B receptor agonist CP-94,253. *Psychopharmacology, 146*, 391-399

Discipline / sub-discipline	Theory / hypothesis	Concept(s)	Assumptions / methodology	Insight into problem
Behavioural neuroscience: The study of physiological and developmental mechanisms of behavior in humans and animals	**Individual differences in brain chemistry can predict behavior:** Psychopathological behavior can be treated clinically with medicine (agonists that mimic naturally occurring substances) based on knowledge of the brain's molecular receptors	**Receptor and agonist:** An agonist is a chemical that binds to a receptor of a cell and triggers a response by the cell. An agonist often mimics the action of a naturally occurring substance	**The treatment works on curtailing this behaviour** Pharmacological agents toward this serotonin-receptor subtype may have more behaviourally specific anti-aggressive effects than those of other current treatments	**Social context also impacts behavior** • The activation of the 5-HT1B serotonin receptor subtype preferentially attenuates heightened aggression due to social instigation or alcohol treatment (in mice) • The social stimuli that precede and occur during an aggressive encounter potently modulate aggressive arousal
Neurochemistry: The study of neurochemicals (molecules such as neurotransmitters) that influence networks of neural operation			**Animal models do not transfer to human trials completely** The 5-HT1B receptors are not identical in rodents and humans, but functionally homologous	**Biological correlates of behavior might explain some differences in aggression between individuals** Neurochemically, aggressive arousal seems to be particularly related to the inhibition of serotonin. Knock-out mice lacking the gene for the 5-HT1B receptor attack faster and have higher frequencies of attack bites
	Genes affect behavior: It has been found that individuals with a genetic predisposition to drink alcohol exhibit tendencies towards impulsive violent behavior		**Genetic modification affects behavior via neurochemicals** Mice, in which the gene that codes for 5-HT1B receptors has been 'knocked out', show aggressive behavior	**The same amount of alcohol affects different people differently** In mice, only a subgroup (20%) show robust and reliable enhancement of aggressive behaviors at 1.0 g/kg dose of alcohol
Genetics: The study of genetic variation, specific genes and heredity in organisms				**Conclusion (insights from mice into the human experience):** There may be a genetic component for aggressive behavior that is elevated by alcohol, and both aggressive behavior and alcohol intake may be influenced by serotonin. Also, linkage has been found between antisocial alcoholics and polymorphisms at the 5-HT 1B gene

Figure 20   Example of a data management table

As you explore the literature, make sure to update your data management table repeatedly throughout the process and to always share it as a team with each other. This not only means that you should keep adding information and insights to your table, but you should also remove irrelevant insights from earlier research phases and keep these in a separate table. Ultimately, your combined data management table will consist of a good coverage of the research topic, including each relevant disciplinary perspective. The items in the table should also make visible to you those places where disciplinary insights are lacking or unclear. It is at this point that students often find a fruitful, focused question for their research to address.

2   Analysis of differences and conflicts

Using a data management table will not only enable you to detect harmonious insights from different disciplines in the literature. Perhaps more importantly, it will help to discover insights that conflict with each other. These conflicting insights can offer you an opportunity for interdisciplinary integration, as you will see below. The following questions can help in finding conflicting and supporting insights:

- Do the insights of different disciplines center around the same topic about which they reveal different aspects?
- Do some of these insights support each other?
- Preferably, insights that support each other should stem from different lines of research and thus rely upon methodological pluralism. For example, children with ADHD have academic difficulties as they have lower average school marks and score lower on attention span tasks.
- In what specific ways do the disciplinary insights contradict or differ from each other?

For example, are the apparent contradictions between results perhaps due to the fact that the insights are derived from studies with different age groups or in different countries? That might point to a developmental influence or a cultural or social one, which might facilitate your more comprehensive interdisciplinary understanding.

Once you have established if there are differences between disciplinary insights, the challenge is to investigate the nature of the differences (after Repko, 2008). One can ask the following questions to discover this:

- Do the disciplinary perspectives use the same concept yet mean something different?
- How are concepts defined and measured?
- Do the different disciplinary theories rest on different assumptions?
- Do these assumptions conflict with each other or can they be seen as complementary?
- Can the conflict between insights be attributed to the different conditions of the research?

In the example of the theoretical analysis of the two articles in the data management table (see box 6), there are tensions between two approaches that rather focus on 'nurture' (social/epidemiological) or on 'nature' (biological/neurological). Questions arise about the extent to which the findings in animal research can be translated to humans (to what extent are the effects of alcohol in the brain of a rat comparable to the effects in a human brain?). Other differences can be found in how aggression is defined and in what amount of alcohol intake is considered problematic. Mind you, this is only a selection of issues that make the insights from the different perspectives at first sight 'incommensurable'. If you were to start scrutinizing the methods (see the chapter on methods), you would find more conflicting operationalizations of concepts and methodological assumptions.

Box 6

Alcohol consumption and aggressive behavior – analysis of the data management table

Suppose that your topic of interest is why alcoholics are often more abusive toward their family members than toward others.

The first article reviews several theories on alcohol-related intimate partner violence among White, Black, and Hispanic partners. Apparently, alcohol consumption goes hand in hand with increases in aggressive behaviour toward partners. It is unclear, however, whether alcohol should be considered the cause of aggression. Certain expectations, individual and relationship history, and environmental factors also seem to play a role when violence occurs.

The authors of the second article discuss social instigation or social stimuli that precede the violence, and they address variants in brain receptors that somehow modulate the level of aggressiveness.

At first glance, the different insights all seem to provide a piece of the puzzle that you are trying to solve. But problems could lurk below the surface, such as:

1 Do both articles adhere to the same concept of violence?
   - Does this match your preconceived definition of violence?
2 What level of alcohol consumption are both articles talking about?
   - How does that compare to the 'alcoholics' you want to study?
3 Do the articles favor the social correlates of violence over the neural correlates, or is it the other way around?
   - In the first article, the level of analysis of brain biochemistry is not considered to be relevant to the behaviour under study. In the second article, however, the social circumstances modulate aggressive arousal in the brain; this modulation is described in biochemical terms, without a mention of individual or social history.
4 Animal studies vs. studies with humans.
   - The second article does experiments with mice, whereas the first deals with human subjects. Are the 'mouse insights' relevant to understanding the human condition?

3   Finding or creating common ground by using integration techniques

Once you have gathered insights into the topic you are researching from all relevant disciplines, it is time to take the first steps toward an interdisciplinary understanding of this topic: what is the common ground between various insights from diverse disciplines? This will form the basis for interdisciplinary integration and also allows you to redefine your main research question in an interdisciplinary way. Remember that such interdisciplinary integration not only involves pertinent techniques but can also require creative imagination for the development of a novel explanatory mechanism, a novel intervention, a novel technology, and so on. We do not have the space here to deal exhaustively with all possible kinds of common ground or all integration techniques that might be used, but hope that our treatment is sufficient to be both helpful and perhaps inspiring for the creative imagination you need as a scientist.

As much as you need to discover an overlap in interests when developing a topic for your interdisciplinary research, you should also try to find common ground when developing an interdisciplinary insight into it. Finding common ground can occur along different lines but often involves: (i) pinpointing a key theory or insight that is somehow shared between disciplines but may be defined and operationalized in different ways; and/or (ii) elaborating an explanatory mechanism by integrating additional insights into it; and/or (iii) making assumptions explicit that might need to be reconsidered by one or more disciplines; and/or (iv) realizing that an existing methodology can perhaps be improved using insights from other disciplines; and/or (v) realizing that the apparently contrasting results from different studies can be reinterpreted in such a way that they are consistent with each other. In some cases, (vi) common ground is created by an existing intervention that must be made more robust by adjusting it in response to a newly uncovered additional factor.

Here are some examples of finding common ground. Some sciences share a common ground right from the beginning in the form of a comprehensive theory, which might need further elaboration in order to explain a particular phenomenon. For example, the theory of quantum mechanics is shared between fields as diverse as astronomy, physics and biology, facilitating to some extent their collaboration. We already discussed how a complex mechanistic explanation allows integration of varied types of explanation. Earlier we also mentioned how economists and sociologists found common ground when they reconsidered the assumption that individuals always maximize their economic self-interest, which made it difficult to explain certain forms of sacrifice or altruism. Contrasting results can sometimes be made consistent with each other once researchers realize that their focus was actually on different developmental stages of a phenomenon or that a particular difference between the study populations was in fact influencing the outcomes in an unexpected manner. Finally, methodologies are often developed within a certain field but turn out to be valuable in others, as when remote sensing has yielded many benefits outside geography in fields like archaeology, astronomy, and sociology.

Although you might have found common ground between disciplines, you should not expect that the tensions between elements of the different disciplines are now completely solved. Instead, it may be useful to focus on these remaining interdisciplinary tensions, as this can lead you to formulate a new question and gain a novel, more comprehensive insight (see box 7). The example on alcohol consumption and aggression presented earlier implies that simply taking the disciplinary insights at face value and building your theoretical framework purely on that basis would lead to a multidisciplinary collage but not to new, integrated interdisciplinary insights. So, although dissecting the nature of differences may feel like a counterintuitive and even counterproductive approach (why would you not focus on where insights overlap or support each other?), focusing on the tensions between research results can provide valuable insights into where common ground can be created.

Especially among the humanities and the social sciences it is more likely that you have to create common ground. This has to do with the theoretical and methodological pluralism that reign in their domains more than in other domains, as mentioned earlier. Harmonious insights are few and differing, whereas conflicting (even diametrically opposed) and incommensurate (when the humanities are added) insights are common. Moreover, in addition to their dependence upon different epistemological assumptions (i.e. if something exists, how can you know that?), these non-harmonious insights usually also stem from different ontological assumptions (what can be said to really exist?) (W.H. Newell, pers. comm., 3 December 2013). Again, such differences between disciplines or specific theories within a discipline regarding their assumptions can offer as many ways to find common ground between them.

Within sociology, for example, authors like Herbert Marcus and Erich Fromm have developed accounts of human society and psychology in which both competing Marxist and psychoanalytical theories were incorporated. The authors dismantled the theories from their exclusivist claims before they could integrate them into accounts of human society and psychology. They argued that a capitalist society with a strong emphasis on consumerism has an impact on the development of certain psychological attitudes in individuals.

Obviously, if one is creating common ground by adjusting the assumptions that underlie certain theories or methods, it is often necessary to reconsider other elements as well. This is due to the fact that many of the ingredients of a science depend upon each other – which is captured by the term 'paradigm' as we have seen above. The challenge is therefore to modify concepts or assumptions as little as possible when bringing out latent commonalities (Newell, 2007).

In this chapter, we have referred to different ways of finding and creating common ground. It is important to realize that, in most cases, we are in fact discussing the different integration techniques that were presented in chapter 6. Remember that these techniques implied that one could use the different techniques of adding, adjusting, or connecting by applying them to scientific theories, methods, or results. We will close this chapter by listing some questions that might help you and your team to embark on this important yet difficult process of finding and creating common ground. You might start to answer these – and more – questions individually and then discuss your answers together, looking for potential connections and overlaps between them.

- Which theories and elements of those theories do you think are most relevant to look into for your research topic?
- Can you discover connections and overlaps of those theories and their elements with those of other disciplines?
- How would you operationalize research into the relevant component(s) or process(es)? How would you study them? What methods, subjects, instruments etc. would you use? Give multiple options if possible.
- Could you articulate the implicit assumptions that are made in your discipline regarding theoretical or methodological elements? Could you imagine different definitions of central concepts, for example? Or would an unusual method of research be potentially interesting?
- What definitions of concepts and elements are central to your approach to the research topic? Do you think that another discipline shares these definitions or might have alternative definitions?
- How do the other disciplines investigate your research topic? Could their methods, subjects, instruments, etc. be added to those of your discipline or are they focusing on different components or processes?
- Do you think that certain components or processes form a coherent subcomponent or, instead, that a certain component should be separated into two or more independent components? Could this explain how the results of a particular study are related to those of a study in another discipline?
- Is there a developmental or historical episode that you think has been neglected while it is relevant for your research topic? Could adding a historical element to an explanatory theory solve this hiatus?
- Similarly, is there a contextual, external, or environmental factor that merits more study as it might have a decisive impact on your research topic?
- Is there a particular intervention that might affect your research topic in a decisive way and that deserves to be better understood?

After having thought about such questions individually and as a group, discuss in your group what you thought of and apply any necessary changes to the map.

Box 7

Different disciplinary definitions: An example

Three students from the fields of biology, cognitive science, and artificial intelligence decided that they wanted to know whether a new monitoring device that could measure stress levels would also be effective in reducing an individual's stress level (Olthof, Bulters & Zwennes, 2011). After reading several articles, they noticed that the concept of 'stress' is defined differently from different disciplinary theoretical perspectives.

From the perspective of artificial intelligence, stress is defined as an objective, measurable factor. The sudden presence of sweat on the skin and an increased heart rate are seen as indicative of stress. Biologists define stress as an external trigger that causes changes in hormone levels and other complex processes that upset 'homeostasis', which are factors that are hard to measure directly. Cognitive science defines stress as a brain state that can occur below the level of conscious perception. Thus, brain states triggered by stressful events are also hard to measure.

From the definitions above, it is possible to see that although stress was a shared concept, it would only provide common ground if the tension between 'externally measurable stress' and 'internal non-measurable processes of stress responses and their interpretation' could be relieved. The research group thus decided that the user of the stress monitor would need to be able to communicate with the stress monitor, for example by temporarily changing settings in hot weather or when doing exercise. AI's assumption that external measurements of stress-related proxies would be objective had to be dropped. Simply monitoring would probably not be sufficient; to be of service in stress reduction both device and human subject are needed in the monitoring process.

In sum, insights derived from different disciplines often appear to be incommensurate, conflicting, or diametrically opposed. The foundation of interdisciplinary integration is the awareness that a discipline operates on specific assumptions, concepts, and theories, and that these differ from discipline to discipline. Through the willingness to embrace 'the new' and the identification of shared concerns, the challenge of interdisciplinary integration can be faced (see the example in box 8).

Interdisciplinary integration in practice: How to speak 'economish'

When Eldar Shafir (Princeton) and Sendhil Mullainathan (Harvard), researchers in psychology and economics, respectively, started to work on a theory of poverty, they spent a lot of time creating a common language. Shafir: "Tolerance, openness, and non-defensiveness of your field are crucial. The goal is to speak the same language, understand each other's issues and perspective. Take Jerry Fodor and Noam Chomsky. They've been talking to each other for so many years that it's hard to say who's the linguist and who's the philosopher" (E. Shafir, pers. comm., 12 December 2013).

As a psychologist, Shafir has invested a lot of time in understanding the economist's perspective. "I wasn't so much interested in the equations; I was trying to figure out what assumptions they had about people. What is the human agent in the eye of the economist? You have to appreciate the other's perspective in order to succeed in interdisciplinary work."

A well-justified transfer of ideas from one discipline to another may also enhance the insights from the disciplines. More practical techniques of integration are also possible; these are discussed later on when we elaborate upon the methodological challenges of conducting interdisciplinary research. Below, in box 9, you will find examples of integration in students' research projects through connecting theories, concepts, and assumptions.

Box 9
Examples of integration in students' research projects

Connecting theories and concepts
Power and dependency

In the field of development studies, power relations and dependencies are often analyzed in an international context, for example through use of dependency theory: A core of wealthy states benefits from resources flowing from peripheral countries, creating an interconnected world system.

In a research project about development and power relations, a student educated in interdisciplinary social sciences connected dependency theory to theories on power from other disciplines. He discovered that power could be analyzed at a global, international level, at an interpersonal level, and at a personal level. These levels are interdependent, meaning the actual effects of power relations at the global level influence the power relations at the interpersonal level, and vice versa. He therefore decided to develop a methodology that would enable him to take these interdependencies into account (Schram, 2012).

Connecting concepts and assumptions
Development and implementation of smart grids

When students were conducting a study into the use of sustainable and efficient electricity networks called smart grids, they realized that the experts in charge of developing and implementing a smart grid system on a student campus were from different disciplines. The economists wanted a solution based on the free market system, the physicists wanted to improve the state of the technology, and the psychologists wanted a solution that promoted human responsibility (Beukenhorst, Huygen & Van Leeuwen, 2012). By placing these assumptions as positions on a scale of possibilities, a spectrum appears: at one end, the state of the art of the technological system dictates the solution, and humans and the market follow; at the other end, the market selects, and humans and technology follow. In the middle, human parties can take responsibility for the development of the technological system and the way selection takes place in the market. So, the place where most of the expertise lies in the provision of the solution depends on the phase of product development and selection.

▼

In response to the incongruences of the solutions posed, the students changed their research question. They now asked what the demands of students (as compared to non-students) are with regard to their use of electricity, and whether they are more motivated by having the latest in technology, by financial stimuli, or by personal values, and what the outcome would mean to the development and implementation of smart grids on campuses. This new approach found common ground in a seemingly divergent problem and provided information that all three groups of experts could use to guide their decision making.

Connecting insights through a mechanistic model
Pelsser's food and behavior diet and ADHD
In order to investigate whether Pelsser's food and behavior diet is more effective than common treatments for ADHD, such as medication and parental training (or a combination of such treatments), three students in psychobiology, politicology, and pedagogy used an existing model from a handbook for the diagnosis and treatment of ADHD (Barkley, 2006) as common ground (Cederhout, Dodu & Perrin, 2012).

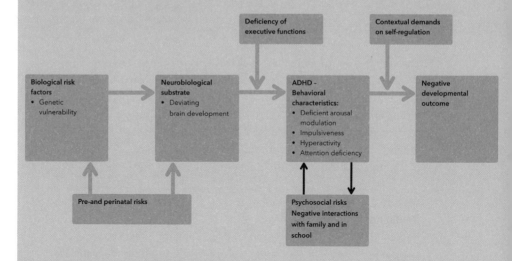

They expanded the model with theories on food-related ADHD and with insights into where in the model the different treatments could be expected to have an effect.

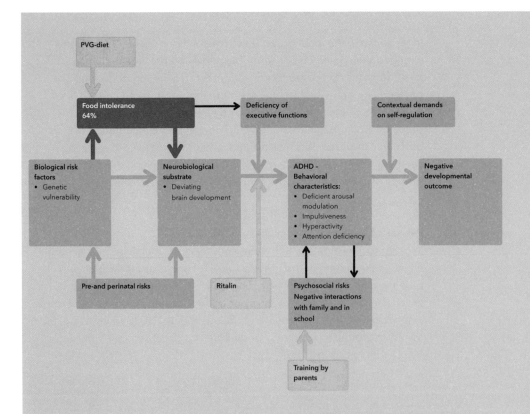

Through this integration, they could refocus their research question, and devise a method by which they reached the conclusion (i.e. new insight). They concluded that although the diet is effective when followed for about a year, and although it has no negative side-effects, only a limited group of children can really benefit from it; these are children in whom ADHD is indeed induced by food and whose parents are sufficiently motivated and disciplined to ensure that their children follow the diet.

Adding or 'borrowing' insights
Redlining and labor mobility
Redlining is a concept that refers to discriminating practices against people from a specific geographical area. An interdisciplinary social sciences student specialized in urban studies found that studies on redlining often try to find out whether it plays a role as a selection criterion in job interviews. She discovered that few studies focused on the perspective of individuals who are subjected to redlining. Combining insights (from human geography) into disadvantaged neighborhoods with theories (from social psychology) on stigmatization at a personal level, enabled her to generate insights into the consequences of redlining (Elands, 2011).

Step 4 Finalize research question

Through the use of one or more integration techniques, you were able to find common ground and develop an integrated theoretical framework. Based on these preliminary insights and the potential common ground between them, you can formulate an interdisciplinary research question, which will form the core of your research project. Make sure your research question is relevant, precise, researchable, and anchored (for more on these criteria, see chapter 9).

It is perhaps superfluous to note, but once your literature research becomes more focused and you have a workable research question, it is still advisable to keep updating your data management table. Along the way, you will find new valuable articles that help to specify and refine your data management table, and may be an incentive for a reformulation of your research question. As mentioned before, interdisciplinary research is an iterative process and it is likely that you will return to your research question and adjust it after every new step you take.

Step 5 Formulate sub-questions

Once you have finalized your research question, you will most likely have to divide this research question into sub-questions. For the sub-questions, the same criteria apply as for the research question (see chapter 9); however, there are some additional factors you have to consider.

There are two main factors you have to consider when developing sub-questions. First, it is important that the intended answers to the sub-questions together lead to an answer to the main research question. Perhaps you need to add another sub-question, if you have discovered that a previously undiscovered property or feature might have an impact upon the topic of your research. Adjust your sub-questions until they cover the finalized research question completely. Second, make sure that your sub-questions are logical steps that lead to your answer. Usually, you can answer one sub-question per paragraph.

For example, when dividing your research question into sub-questions, you can decide to divide a concept into terms that can be measured more easily. In the example on fogponics (chapter 13), the finalized research question 'To what extent can fogponics contribute to a more sustainable form of greenhouse cultivation?' is sub-divided into two questions:

- Is fogponics a better alternative in terms of efficient nutrient use when compared to conventional greenhouse agriculture?
- Is fogponics a better alternative in terms of efficient water use when compared to conventional greenhouse agriculture?

The sub-questions themselves can be divided into questions. In the example of fogponics one could research per nutrient whether fogponics or conventional greenhouse agriculture is a better alternative. However, be careful not to go overboard in sub-dividing your sub-questions, as this can lead to results that are redundant or too specific.

10 How to collect and analyze your data

After reviewing the relevant literature from the disciplines that were identified as being essential for addressing your initial research question, you have developed a theoretical framework that enabled you to refine the research question. Now, the question is, how are you going to answer this refined research question? It is time to develop a methodological framework for data collection and data analysis.

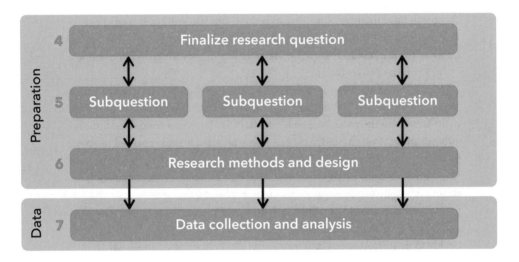

Figure 21   Steps 4, 5, 6 and 7 of the IIS model for interdisciplinary research

Considerations:
- What are the relevant methods each discipline has to offer? Is a combination of methods possible?
- How does the choice of methods influence the results?

Step 6   Develop research methods and design

The process of developing such a methodological framework to structure the practical matters of your research project is similar to the process you used to develop a theoretical framework to define the theoretical context and specify the focus of your research. This methodological framework is what we call 'the design' of your research. The process of translating your research questions into practical researchable questions is what we call 'operationalization', which has already been discussed in the context of the Science Cycle (chapter 2). This part of the research process is highlighted in figure 21.

In this chapter, we will guide you through the process of developing an adequate and manageable methodological framework. You have to ask yourself the following guiding questions during this step of the research process:

1   What (kind of) information is required in order to answer the research question?
2   What approach is the most appropriate for answering the research question?
3   Which methods are the most appropriate for producing the data needed?

Below we will elaborate more on these questions.

1   **What (kind of) information is required in order to answer the research question?**
The question you are trying to answer can take many forms. It can, for example, be an observational or experimental question, but might also be a question that leads to problem solving. The starting point can also be a prediction or a hypothesis instead of a question. In any case, you will have to unravel different features that are relevant with regard to the problem, prediction, or hypothesis in order to be able to answer or test it. Therefore, you first need to divide it into sub-questions. These sub-questions can be either disciplinary or interdisciplinary. For example, to what extent is aggressive behavior caused by a failure of self-control? And how is alcohol use modifying such self-control? Is behavioral self-control comparable to cognitive self-control?

Furthermore, your question and sub-questions contain concepts that you need to operationalize, and you therefore need to define exactly what you mean by these concepts. For example, when you are researching aggressive behavior, you should first define it and distinguish it from, for instance, assertive behavior. If you aim to focus on behavioral self-control, then you might need to operationalize how you aim to study this in practice and what standards you will be using. In other words, you are developing one or more ways for translating relevant concepts into researchable items (see also chapter 2). Since interdisciplinary research is often exploring new fields, existing methods are not always sufficient to operationalize your research question. That is why creativity is very important during this phase of the research project.

To operationalize your research question, it can be very useful, if not essential, to look into the possibilities of integrating the research approaches, methods, or techniques that are rooted in different disciplines. There are several possible techniques to integrate different approaches, methods, or techniques. Just as we saw in the previous chapter, you need to consider the type of change you need to make to existing methods and techniques in order to be able to find results with which you can answer your integrated research question. You may need to add an extra measuring technique, adjust a specific method, or connect different methods and techniques with each other (see figure 22).

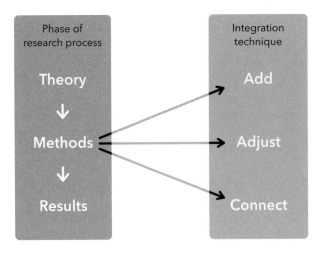

Figure 22   *Possible integration techniques at the level of methodology*

2   What approach is the most appropriate to answer the research question?
The way you translate theories and concepts into a useful operationalization depends on your approach. As we saw in chapter 1, there are different ways of thinking about knowledge and how knowledge should and can be gained. The approach you take can be positivistic and quantitative, or interpretative and qualitative, or, especially in the case of interdisciplinary research, a combination of both (i.e. a mixed methods approach). In many cases, it is only through a combination of approaches that one is able to get to a more complete understanding (see also methodological pluralism, as introduced in chapter 2). The approach you use also depends on the kind of question you ask. In the case of interdisciplinary research, it is often worthwhile considering using different approaches at the same time.

3   Which methods are the most appropriate to produce the data needed?
There are different ways to find an answer to this question, and the answer you find will depend, to some extent, on the operationalization you have chosen and the methods and techniques that you will use. For example, the results of a specific qualitative case study will differ from a quantitative comparative study into the same topic, but there will be some kind of correspondence between the two. An interdisciplinary goal would be to integrate these results irrespective of their methodological differences: probably the qualitative insights might help us to adjust our questionnaires and thus contribute to enhanced quantitative research.
To find out what the customary methods and techniques are in different disciplines, it is wise to return to your data management table (see figure 18). The table provides a brief overview of the articles you have read and analyzed so far, and you can learn from these articles how the key concepts have been operationalized in the different theoretical frameworks. You then have to decide with what adaptation or combination of these methodologies you can perform your own research.

Preferences for specific methods are common within disciplines. But if you perform research into a problem that crosses disciplinary boundaries, a combination of techniques often offers more accurate results. Furthermore, you might consider using your knowledge of and skills in a disciplinary method that is new to a particular problem.

It is perfectly possible that a technique used in discipline A cannot be used in the exact same way in discipline B. In that case, you might need to adjust the technique. Another possibility can be the adjustment of a specific theory and to use it as input for a data gathering technique in another field. In box 10 you will find examples of student projects where integration took place after methods or techniques were added, adjusted, or connected.

The choice of method, the practical limitations of methods, and the time allotted for your research may force you to reconsider your research question and adapt it to the research means. This is part of the iterative process that is inherent to interdisciplinary research. Adapting to the possibilities is challenging but unavoidable, so do not get discouraged too easily. Just be mindful that you might have to modify your research question because of practical limitations, and that this generally means you are moving forwards, not backwards!

Box 10
Examples of integration at the level of methods

Add a method
The influence of stress on human decision-making
Suppose you want to understand the influence of stress on human decision-making. Then you might consider using a device that measures the galvanic skin response under different test conditions (which conditions depends on the focus of your concrete research question) in order to get quantitative data on the physiological state of arousal, which can then be taken as a proxy for the stress level. But because this device cannot measure the subjective mental experience that accompanies the state of arousal, you might want to add a more qualitative type of measurement to differentiate between different mental states, like a short questionnaire (Maan, Cupido & van Moll, 2012).

Connecting methods
Measuring the weight of the dodo
In historical images of the dodo, this extinct bird is sometimes pictured as rather heavy, and sometimes as rather skinny. In addition, its weight was unknown. In their data management table, four students (van Dierendonck, van Egmond, ten Hagen & Kreuning, 2013) found that in

▼

many different methods were used to reconstruct the weight of the dodo. They past research, found differences in the reference species that was used (in other words: to which non-extinct bird species the dodo was compared), differences in the type of bones that were used as an indicator to determine overall weight of the animal, and differences in which part of the bone was measured. The students integrated elements of these research methods and their underlying assumptions into a new method, with which they were able to assess the dodo's weight more accurately.

Adding and connecting methods

Development of tumors

The development of tumors is usually the object of study for medical scientists. However, in their research project on tumor development, three students in psychobiology, medical biology, and econometrics learned that the behavior of tumor cells can also be studied from an economics perspective.

They used evolutionary game theory to create a model to describe and explain the behavior of tumor cells. Through the introduction of a way of studying that was new to the medical sciences, they found a new explanation for the development of tumors. This new information might offer new ways of fighting tumors by means of influencing the interaction between developing tumor cells (Dijkgraaf, Hooghiemstra & van der Spoel, 2009).

Adding and connecting theory and method

Volunteer tourism in Cuzco

During a research project on volunteer tourism in Cuzco, an interdisciplinary social scientist (Schram, 2012) wanted to learn more about how the different actors in volunteer tourism experience the power relations, and also how they evaluate the dependencies they experience. Interviewing relevant actors seems an appropriate research method. However, thoughts and feelings about power relations often appear to be part of a bigger narrative. Moreover, individuals are not always aware of their attitude toward it. It is therefore hard, if not impossible, to get relevant answers from actor interviews about these topics.

Positioning theory (from the field of social psychology) gives an explanation about how people define the 'self' in conversations. In his research project, Schram used the knowledge gained from positioning theory to improve the interview method: respondents were asked to write on Post-it notes the different groups of actors that, according to them, are involved in volunteer tourism in Cuzco. They were then asked to put the notes in two different orders:

▼

from least influence to most influence, and from independent to dependent. In this way, the positioning theory was used as a method in the domain of social interactions and it was thereby possible to gain insights into the way individuals perceive power relations.

Adjusting techniques for data analysis
Omega-3 fatty acid and heart rate variability
In order to find the impact of omega-3 fatty acid intake on heart rate variability (HRV) in men and women, two students with backgrounds in biomedical sciences and mathematics realized that first they had to look into the way HRV was being analyzed. They found the current technique to be outdated and they introduced a new technique for the analysis of HRV: the mathematical logarithm ApEn. This new technique and the use of an existing dataset allowed them to determine the influence of omega-3 fatty acid intake on the HRV in men and women with more accuracy. In this project, the analysis method of one discipline (mathematics) affected the data acquisition of another discipline (cardiology), as a slightly different data set was requested from cardiologists (Bekius & Elsenburg, 2010).

Step 7 Data collection and analysis

When you have selected a (disciplinary) method, you also commit to the standard (disciplinary) criteria and standards to collect and analyze data with that method. However, when you have translated or adjusted a method or technique, this may mean you have to reconsider your methods of data collection and analysis and possibly adjust them, without negatively affecting the validity, reliability, and accuracy of the method (see the Omega-3 fatty acid and heart rate variability example in Box 10).

A first step in data analysis is checking the raw data. Some of your data may simply not be useful or false (for example as a consequence of a mistake in an experiment). Suppose that you used survey questionnaires as a method for data collection and asked about the age of the participants. If somebody filled in '763 years old', you know this cannot be true and you have to adjust the otherwise skewed results.

In some cases you need to categorize, or code your data. There are different techniques for coding data and, as mentioned previously, the technique you choose depends on the kind of data you collected and the goal and approach of your research. If you use a quantitative approach, your data should be coded in a way that allows you to perform statistical analysis. For example, if you asked participants about work satisfaction and the possible answers to choose from were 'not satisfied', 'more or less satisfied' and 'very satisfied', you need to label these categories with different numbers before you can use them in statistical analyses. If you use a qualitative approach, you should also code your data. You need to think about the themes or variables you want to use to analyze and mark different parts of your data that correspond with that theme or variable, before you can interpret the data set. It is possible and even advisable to use multiple techniques to analyze the same data. Integration of different data analysis techniques might actually improve the quality of your research project and the robustness of its outcomes.

After you have checked and coded the data, performed statistical analysis of different variables, and/or described the meaning of different themes within your data, it is time to connect different variables and themes. In order to do this, you need to explain how different themes and variables are related to each other. If you used both qualitative and quantitative analysis of the same data, you need to bring together the findings resulting from both analyses. You also need to think about the way you are going to present or visualize the data or findings. This can be done by means of graphs and/or tables, but there are numerous other ways. Note that in different disciplines, different ways to visualize the data are the norm. Especially when carrying out interdisciplinary research as a team, communication of the results is key, not only to the outside world, but also within the research team. Therefore, it is important to look for the optimal way of visualizing your data, in a way that is understandable across the involved disciplines. Eventually, this information should enable you to answer your sub-questions.

11 Discussion and conclusion(s)

Now that you have analyzed your data, it is time to discuss your results and reach a conclusion. You must first decide which technique to use to integrate your results. Once you have integrated them, your results will either verify or falsify the hypothesis (or hypotheses) you have been testing. To wrap up the story, it is helpful for the reader if you reiterate your research process by retracing and sharing your steps. Note that the order in which the discussion and conclusion(s) are presented in research papers differs from discipline to discipline and from journal to journal. In our model we place the discussion before the conclusion(s) (figure 23).

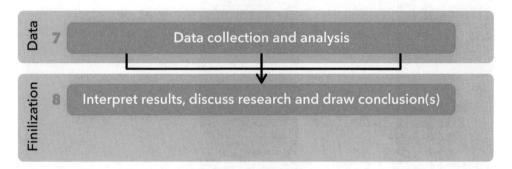

Figure 23   Steps 7 and 8 of the IIS model for interdisciplinary research

Considerations:
- Do the results confirm your hypothesis or expectations from your integrated theoretical framework?
- Does your interdisciplinary insight (or solution) shed new light on the insights obtained by each discipline separately?
- Spell out to your readers, who will often be disciplinary scientists – how specific disciplinary insights have been integrated into your interdisciplinary conclusion and, conversely, how this might have an impact on their future disciplinary research.
- What parts of your interdisciplinary research may be sensitive to criticism, and why?
- Based on your results, what research question would you want to pose next?

Step 8   Interpret results, discuss research & draw conclusion(s)

In chapter 6 we showed that integration can be conducted at multiple levels or at multiple locations in a complex system or mechanism. During this final step of the research process, it is often a matter of connecting results, rather than adding elements or adjusting them, although it is likely that you will end up combining all of them during the analysis (see box 11). Integration of results is usually necessary in the case of optimization problems. Furthermore, integration of results takes place when research leads to practical solutions or products. The conclusions of your research project are likely to raise new questions. Based on those new questions you can give recommendations for future research.

Creating a conceptual model can be a way to visualize and integrate your results (like the example on fisheries in box 4 on p. 47). With such a model, you are able to give an orderly representation of the system or problem you have researched. Consequently, you can uncover interactions between different aspects of the problem that are typically addressed by different disciplines

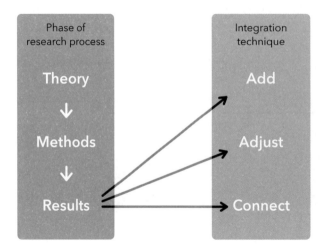

Figure 24   Possible integration techniques at the level of results

Box 11

Example of integration at the level of results

Connect and optimize results

Finding the optimal location for the generation of sustainable energy in Mexico

A group of three students (van Dun, Muller & Boeke 2012) carried out a study on sustainable energy in Mexico. They found that given the amount of wave energy in the seas surrounding Mexico, the generation of offshore wave energy appears to be a promising technique. However, in order to generate and distribute energy properly, a stable political situation is essential. So, to give an answer to the question how wave energy can be best implemented in Mexico, both natural sciences (physics and earth science) and social sciences (political science) are necessary. They first analyzed in which regions of Mexico the most energy is used, and then mapped the degree of social and political stability in these regions. It turned out that the optimal location in terms of energy yield did not match the optimal location with regards to political stability. So, it ultimately came down to optimization between the regions with the highest amount of wave energy and the most stable political situation (van Dun et al., 2012).

At the beginning of the research project, you started with a problem, which you then narrowed down into a research question and sub-questions. Subsequently, you chose methods to answer your main question and sub-questions. In this process of specifying the problem, you likely have made several choices, which may have forced you to reconsider choices you made in previous steps. In order to formulate a well-considered discussion, you need to reflect on all the choices you made throughout the project that might have influenced the results.

But the first task at hand is to answer your research question. The following questions form a guideline that may help you structure the discussion/conclusions chapter.

- Why did you need an interdisciplinary perspective – i.e. what were likely shortcomings of disciplinary perspectives?
- What was your research question?
- From the perspective of the integrated, interdisciplinary theoretical framework that you have prepared, what answer(s) did you expect?
- What results did you find?
- How do you interpret these results in the context of your theoretical framework?
- What repercussions could your research and conclusion have for those disciplinary perspectives involved in your study?
- What advice for further disciplinary studies could you draw from this?

Even if the results completely confirm your hypothesis, it is always possible to discuss the choices and interpretations you made during the research process. Also, your results are often supported by previous research, but there are likely results that do not necessarily warrant as conclusions. Do not ignore those alternative explanations, but give them a place in your discussion. In other words, discuss your results in the context of the total coverage of the literature. Also, articulate and reflect upon the limitations of your study's methods – and suggest possible follow-up studies. When discussing your study, you could, for example, answer the following questions:

- Does your method/or do your methods contain elements that leave room for alternative explanations?
- Are there alternative points of view from which your results could be interpreted in a different way?

Up to this point, your conclusion and discussion chapter is not really very different from one you would find in a disciplinary paper, except that the information is provided by multiple academic disciplines. However, there is more to reflect upon: the interdisciplinary research process you followed and the surplus value of your interdisciplinary approach.

- Did the interdisciplinary research process lead to unexpected insights? If so, where did they occur?
- Were these insights into the main research question, or tangential to your line of inquiry?
- Were there steps specified in the model on interdisciplinary research provided by this manual that did not fit the project well? If so, how did you adjust the process?
- Overall, what did you learn about the interdisciplinary process?
- Do your interdisciplinary insights shed new light on the individual insights from each discipline? Or can your insights be criticized for lacking depth or being too reductionist?
- Has your analysis perhaps unearthed some important issues that deserve more attention?
- Which gaps in knowledge still exist and, moreover, which gaps in knowledge have surfaced as a result of the insights provided by your research?
- What opportunities do you see for new research (directions)?

You may also include tips for improvement as you consider the approach you have chosen, as well as making suggestions for future research as you draw your paper to a close.

You have now taken all the steps that eventually led to an interdisciplinary answer to your integrated research question. You have brought together different disciplinary insights and integrated them in order to get a more complete and inclusive understanding of the complex problem you have researched. It is now time to write a report on your interdisciplinary research. In this report, it is also important to systematically reflect on your research, which poses new questions. Note that this is more complex in the case of interdisciplinary science, as you not only address future interdisciplinary research, but also inspire disciplinary science that relates to your research topic. Therefore, it is important to be aware of the fact that you are not targeting a specific audience, but rather appeal to a diverse audience consisting of both disciplinary and interdisciplinary academics. It is your task to give suggestions for both future disciplinary research as well as interdisciplinary research. So, this is where you also point out what the relevance of this particular interdisciplinary research project is for 'normal science'.

References

Abma, R. (2011). *Over de Grenzen van Disciplines – Plaatsbepaling van de Sociale Wetenschappen*. Nijmegen: Uitgeverij Vantilt.

Barkley, R. (2006). *Attention Deficit Hyperactivity Disorder: A Handbook for Diagnosis and Treatment* (3rd ed.). New York: The Guilford Press.

Berkes, F. (2003). Alternatives to conventional management: Lessons from small-scale fisheries. *Environments, 31*, 5-19.

Caetano, R., Schafer, J. & Cunradi, C.B. (2001). Alcohol-related intimate partner violence among white, black, and Hispanic couples in the United States. *Alcohol Research & Health, 25*, 58-65.

Chalmers, A.F. (1999). *What is this Thing called Science?* Maidenhead: Open University Press.

Charles, A.T. (1994). Towards sustainability: the fishery experience. *Ecological Economics, 11*, 201-211.

Cooper, J. M. (ed.) (1997). *Plato; Complete Works*. Cambridge: Hackett Publishing Company.

Eigenbrode, S.D., O'Rourke, M., Wulfhorst, J.D., Althoff, D.M., Goldberg, C.S., et al. (2007). Employing philosophical dialogue in collaborative science. *BioScience, 57*, 55-64.

Fish, E.W, Faccidomo, S. & Miczek, K.A. (1999). Aggression heightened by alcohol or social instigation in mice: reduction by the 5-HT B receptor agonist CP-94,253. *Psychopharmacology, 146*, 391-399.

Frodeman, R., Klein, J.T. & Mitcham, C. (eds.) (2010). *The Oxford Handbook of Interdisciplinarity*. Oxford: Oxford University Press.

Garcia, S.M. & Cochrane, K.L. (2005). Ecosystem approach to fisheries: A review of implementation guidelines. *ICES Journal of Marine Science, 62*, 311-318.

Hirsch-Hadorn, G., Hoffmann-Riem, H., Biber-Klemm S., Grossenbacher-Mansuy, W., Joye, D., et al. (eds.) (2008). *Handbook of transdisciplinary research*. Dordrecht: Springer.

Holland, J.H. (2006). Studying complex adaptive systems. *Journal of Systems Science and Complexity, 19*, 1-8.

Le Treut, H., Somerville, R., Cubasch, U., Ding, Y., Mauritzen, C., et al. (2007). Historical overview of climate change. In: S. Solomon, D. Qin, M. Manning, Z. Chen, M. Marquis, et al. (eds.), *Climate Change 2007: The Physical Science Basis. Contribution of Working Group I to the Fourth Assessment Report of the Intergovernmental Panel on Climate Change* (p. 93-127). Cambridge: Cambridge University Press.

Jury, W.A. & Vaux, H. Jr. (2005). The role of science in solving the world's emerging water problems. *Proceedings of the National Academy of Sciences of the USA, 44*, 15715–15720.

Keestra, M. (2012). Understanding Human Action – Integrating Meanings, Mechanisms, Causes, and Contexts. In: A.F. Repko, W.H. Newell & R. Szostak (eds.), *Case Studies in Interdisciplinary Research* (p. 225-258). Thousand Oaks, CA: Page Publications.

Klein, J.T. & Newell, W. (1997). Advancing interdisciplinary studies. In: J. G. Gaff & J. Ratcliff (eds.), *Handbook of the Undergraduate Curriculum* (p. 393-394). San Francisco: Jossey-Bass.

Klein, J.T. (1990). *Interdisciplinarity – History, Theory and Practice*. Detroit: Wayne State University Press.

Krishnan, A. (2009). *What are Academic Disciplines? Some Observations on the Disciplinarity vs. Interdisciplinarity Debate* (ESRC national centre for research methods working paper series 03/09). Southampton: University of Southampton.

Lélé, S. & Norgaard, R.B. (2005). Practicing interdisciplinarity. *BioScience, 55*, 967–975.

Levin, S.A. (1998). Ecosystems and the biosphere as complex adaptive systems. *Ecosystems, 1*, 431–436.

Mann, M.E., Bradley, R.S. & Hughes, M.K. (1999). Northern hemisphere temperatures during the past millennium: inferences, uncertainties, and limitations. *Geophysical Research Letters, 26*, 759-762.

Mitchell, M. (2009). *Complexity – A Guided Tour*. New York: Oxford University Press.
National Academy of Sciences (2005). *Facilitating Interdisciplinary Research*.
Washington: The National Academies Press.

National Science Foundation (2001). *NSF GPRA Strategic Plan FY 2001–2005*.
Arlington, VA: National Science Foundation.

Newell, W.H. (2006). Interdisciplinary integration by undergraduates. *Issues in Integrative Studies, 24*, 89-111.

Newell, W.H. (2007). Chapter 13 "Decision making in interdisciplinary studies". In:
Göktug Morçöl (ed.) *Handbook of Decision Making in Interdisciplinary Studies* (p.
245-264). New York: CRC Press/Taylor & Francis Group.

Page, S.E. (2010). *Diversity and Complexity*. Princeton, NJ: Princeton University
Press.

Paul, R. & Elder, L. (2014). *The Miniature Guide to Critical Thinking Concepts and
Tools*. Tomales, CA: The Foundation for Critical Thinking.

Popper, K.R. (1963). *Conjectures and Refutations: The Growth of Scientific
Knowledge*. London: Routledge.

Repko, A.F. (2007). Integrating interdisciplinarity: How the theories of common
ground and cognitive interdisciplinarity are forming the debate on interdisciplinary
integration. *Issues in Integrative Studies, 25*, 1-31.

Repko, A.F. (2012). *Interdisciplinary Research – Process and Theory (2nd edition)*.
Thousand Oaks, CA: Sage Publications.

Rittel, H.W.J. & Webber, M.M. (1973). Dilemmas in a general theory of planning.
Policy Sciences, 4, 155-169.

Salisbury, F. & Ross, C. (1985). *Plant Physiology*. Belmont, CA: Wadsworth
Publishing Company.

van Santen, R.A., Khoe, D. & Vermeer, B. (2010). *2030 – Technology that will Change
the World*. New York: Oxford University Press.

Scheffer, M., Carpenter, S., Foley, J.A., Folke, C. & Walker, B. (2001). Catastrophic
shifts in ecosystems. *Nature, 4*, 591-596.

Talisayon, S.D. (2010, March 28). Group Mind Mapping. *Apin Talisayon's weblog*.
Consulted on https://apintalisayon.wordpress.com/

Valli, K. (2011). Dreaming in the multilevel framework. *Consciousness and Cognition, 20*, 1084-1090.

World Commission on Environment and Development (1987). *Our Common Future*. Oxford: Oxford University Press.

Part 2
From 'Academic Skills for Interdisciplinary Studies'

1 Preparatory reading and searching

When you start an academic project – whether it's a research study or a degree course – it is important to learn how to familiarize yourself with a topic well. Preparatory reading plays a key part in this.

You'll need three things for this. First of all, you need to select a particular research field by familiarizing yourself broadly with a topic. Second, you need scholarly knowledge, so that you can also familiarize yourself with the academic aspects of your chosen research field. And third, from this seemingly endless amount of information, you need to be able to extract the information you find interesting and that will help you to focus on the problem you will eventually investigate.

Familiarizing yourself with a topic

It's best to **familiarize yourself with a discipline or topic** as broadly as possible by looking beyond academia. Finding a topic is not always easy; some people have a whole raft of ideas to get working on, whereas others can take days or even weeks to come up with the right one. A few tips:

- Be enthusiastic, but not unrealistic. It goes without saying that you should choose a topic that fires your enthusiasm, but when making your selection, consider your options carefully – mainly in terms of time, but also in terms of skills. You won't be expected to publish any revolutionary findings in a first-year paper. In most cases, a small and well-defined topic is interesting (and complex) enough. For example, you might be tempted to throw yourself into finding out to what extent an entire economy has become circular, but it may already be challenging and tricky enough to find out which building materials are being recycled in the construction sector, and in what ways.
- Be open-minded, but beware of cul-de-sacs. One of the aims of a university degree course and/or research is to generate creative and innovative research, so you should be open to new dimensions, new methods, and yet-to-be-explored topics – but beware of drifting too far from the mainstream. If you do, you may find yourself in a cul-de-sac: a dead end that is difficult to escape. Many exciting-sounding social developments and/or innovations still lack large-scale applications, and often little research has been done on them. It is unlikely that you, someone who is just starting out, will be able to contribute much. You should always find out first whether enough is known about a topic already, or you might find yourself wasting a lot of time on it.

- Be creative, but stay close to the assignment. First-year students are often set assignments in which they learn particular skills that are tested later. Although you need to be creative when using your research skills, make sure that you don't lose sight of the objective. This starts with the topic itself; if one learning objective of the assignment is to carry out a survey, it isn't helpful to choose a topic for which you need to find respondents on the other side of the world.

Finding your bearings outside the university

In some cases, the assignment includes a list of potential topics; in others, you are free to choose your own topic. In both cases, though, you need to decide exactly what you're going to research. Scholarly research almost invariably starts with an *observation*: something that catches your eye or fascinates you. Such observations can be made anywhere, meaning that there are no limits to the source of inspiration.

One place where you can look for inspiration is *current events*. Start your search with something that has sparked your interest – perhaps something you recently saw or read. The advantage of being an interdisciplinary student is that you often have great freedom in your choice of topic, as you're not limited by disciplinary boundaries. Current events are covered by countless media sources and platforms. You could look at newspapers, television programmes, and social media platforms, of course. In particular, *documentaries* and *TV programmes* with an investigative approach (such as the BBC's *Panorama* programme) can frame topics nicely. *Magazines* such as *Time*, *Prospect*, or *The Economist* are good places for finding short, in-depth analyses of particular topics.

You could also look at popular scientific journals (see 'Other useful sources' at the end of this chapter). Sometimes, you can take inspiration from *museums and exhibitions*; in the field of modern art in particular, links are often drawn with current events and social developments, and sometimes even directly with science and technology.

Finding your bearings at university

The university world can often feel (and can be) massive and impersonal, but this doesn't mean that it is impossible to make personal contacts or develop a network. Many successful academic careers have started this way. Not only can lecturers and researchers serve as interesting subjects of study, but they can also act as very helpful guides in the diffuse landscape of the university.

Although professors and lecturers tend to be extremely busy, they are often enthusiastic about motivated and smart students who are interested in their research field. For this reason, they are often prepared to discuss ideas with you, even if they do not teach you personally. You do need to approach them with *focused questions*, though, and not just general talk such as: 'Do you know of a good topic for me?' In many cases, a good starting point is the scholar themselves. Do a search on them in a search engine, take a look at their university web page, read recent publications, and search for any events, lectures, and blogs they might be involved with. Perhaps this will give rise to new search terms, domains, or lecturers, which will help you to continue your search.

Finding your bearings between university and society

As well as current events, you could also consider social and scholarly debates (or a mix of the two), where you can browse topics to your heart's content. *Lectures and debates* are frequently organized by the university (or by foundations with academic links). Lectures are often a good opportunity to familiarize yourself with a particular academic field. What's more, debates often showcase socially relevant topics that are discussed from multiple angles. In most university towns, you'll come across organizations that hold regular lectures, debates, and thematic evenings, often in partnership with or organized by university lecturers and professors. If you're interested in transdisciplinary research where academic knowledge and practical knowledge come together, this is certainly a useful place to start your search.

An initial literature search

Once you've selected your topic, it is important to get a rapid, thorough overview of the key publications, what these publications show, and which gaps still exist in the academic knowledge. The objective of a literature review is to find academic sources that help you to map out the concepts, theories, and empirical studies that are relevant to your topic. This objective is two-fold. On the one hand, you want to find out as much as you can about your research field. On the other hand, you also want to tap into unexplored fields, in order to find your own particular research topic.

You therefore need to come up with keywords and search terms based on the topic you're interested in, which can be used to find useful literature. As you do this, it's important to understand what lies at the heart of scholarship; in other words, what concepts and theories are. And second, you need to know exactly what a scholarly article is. Finally, you need to know which databases are available and how to use them.

Concepts and theories

Concepts and theories form the bedrock of all scholarship. They are a key fixture in the humanities and social sciences, and are often referred to as such; but natural scientists also use concepts and theories, consciously or not. **Theories** are supposed relationships between concepts. A **concept** is an abstraction, supposed pattern, or idea that can be defined or combined in different ways. This supposed relationship between concepts can take the form of a **correlation**, when you see a link between two concepts; for example, if concept A is measured somewhere, and concept B is also measured. However, if you can make a reasonable case that concept A can *explain* the presence of concept B (in other words, that A leads to B), this is known as a **causal relationship** (Walliman, 2011). Concepts are thus the building blocks of theories.

To give an example of a causal relationship (cause-effect): a scholar might hypothesize that the increase in social media (concept 1) is leading to a digitally dependent culture (concept 2). In this case, 'increase in social media' and 'digitally dependent culture' are concepts that can be used to describe and explain reality. Demonstrating a causal relationship is tricky, though, because it is hard to exclude the possibility that this is only a correlation – and it would be wrong to presume a causal relationship purely on the basis of a correlation. How wrong? See *Figure 1.1*! To return to the claim that the 'increase in social media' is leading to a 'digitally dependent culture', what if a third concept, 'technological progress', were to explain both the 'increase in social media' and our 'digitally dependent culture'? Or perhaps our digitally dependent culture is leading to an increase in social media?

Figure 1.1 There is a correlation between the number of films that feature the actor Nicolas Cage and the number of people who drown in swimming pools each year, but this doesn't mean that there is a causal relationship between the two - that is, that one causes the other. Source: Vigen (n.d.)

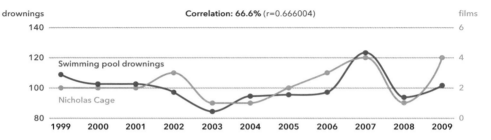

Theories and concepts also play a major role in research in the natural sciences. Underlying seemingly neutral terms such as 'soil quality' and 'ecosystem services' are complex discussions about how these should be defined. This means that definitions (and theories about the supposed relationships between them) can differ significantly across the disciplines and between scholars. One scholar might define 'poverty' as 'having to live on less than 1 euro a day', for example, whereas another might define it as 'the absence of sanitary facilities'. And when it comes to the relationship between 'criminality' and 'poverty', it makes a big difference whether you define 'criminality' as the 'number of burglaries' or 'fraud'. Everything stands or falls with how concepts are defined and how they are thought to relate to one other, and it is also crucial how these concepts and theories are operationalized (made measurable; more on this in Part 2) and eventually used in a research study.

All of this might sound complicated and abstract, but now it's time for the good news: concepts and theories simultaneously act as beacons that can guide you through your university career. Focusing on concepts and theories will allow you to find your bearings rapidly in a new academic field (see the rest of this chapter), cut to the heart of a text, draw useful links between several texts (*Chapter 2*), and help you to organize the information that you need easily (*Chapter 3*). What's more, focusing on concepts and theories will help you to formulate a theoretical framework, define your problem clearly, and, ultimately, come up with a pertinent, well-defined research question (see *Part 2*). You will also use concepts and theories when you construct a research instrument and when analysing your results (see *Part 3*). In short, if the core theme of this book is research practice, then concepts and theories are the core theme that runs through research practice, as it were.

Scholarly literature

All scholarly articles therefore contain concepts and theories, but we can also recognize academic texts through other characteristics. Scholars produce various kinds of texts, which differ from other texts in a number of respects. If you are reading for research purposes, it is important to be able to distinguish non-academic sources from academic ones.

Although texts in different academic disciplines can differ significantly in terms of structure, form, and length, almost all academic articles (research articles and literature reports) share a number of characteristics:

- They are published in **scholarly journals** with expert editorial boards. An example of a well-known journal in the natural sciences is *Nature*; a highly valued scholarly journal in the social sciences is the *Journal of Political Economy*; and *Poetics* is a highly regarded journal in the humanities (especially in the field of literature).
  - One way to measure a journal's value is its **impact factor**. This is based on the number of citations of its articles in other scholarly articles, with the reasoning that an oft-cited article must be groundbreaking and important in its field. A good overview of journal impact factors can be found in the Web of Science's journal citation reports.
- These journals are **peer-reviewed**, which means that their content is assessed by at least two independent and usually anonymous scholars (see *Chapter 13* for more on peer review). If you are unsure whether a journal is peer-reviewed or not, you can always Google it (search for the name of the journal and 'peer-reviewed').
- These articles are written by authors who have no direct commercial or political interest in the topic on which they are writing, and the authors' background is always given (often including their contact details, which can be found at the beginning of the article). Many articles include the statement: 'The authors declare that there is no conflict of interest'.

- Articles are often preceded by an **abstract**: a concise summary of the key findings, the context and the implications of the research (see *Chapter 10* for more on drafting abstracts).
- Articles contain a large number of **references** to other scholarly publications on the same topic. The references are often in the text, either at the end or in the middle of sentences. In addition, all of the references are provided in a bibliography at the end of the article (see *Chapter 11*).

In short, **scholarly literature** can be distinguished from 'ordinary' literature because the degree of objectivity and reliability is guaranteed, it is closely monitored by the academic community, and the authors themselves have no commercial or political interest in the topic. In *Chapters 1 and 2*, we delve more deeply into the different kinds of academic literature and the various strategies that you can use to read it.

Grey literature

In addition to academic literature, you will come across **grey literature**. These are publications written by researchers or research organizations, but they are not peer-reviewed. There is thus no guarantee that the content of these studies has been checked by specialists. Nevertheless, you will often read such texts, because they frequently contain specialized and specific knowledge that is not available in academic publications.

Grey literature derives its name from the fact that it occupies the 'grey area' between academic and non-academic literature. For this reason, it is often difficult to gauge whether these articles are of sufficient quality to be used as reliable sources. They include **advisory reports**, sometimes by organizations on their own performance, and sometimes by consultancies on other organizations and external projects. Often, you will need to look carefully at the independence (or otherwise) of these reports. Who funded them and who has an interest in what outcome? There are also **non-academic research reports** such as UN reports, data from statistics institutes, and government reports. Although these are not, strictly speaking, peer-reviewed, the reliability of these sources means that their contents can be assumed to be valid. Despite this, it is a good idea to use academic sources alongside these sources. Finally, you will come across **non-academic (or yet-to-become academic) publications from the academic world**. They include theses, such as Master's and Bachelor's theses, and doctoral research that is ongoing or that hasn't yet been published in academic journals. You should be critical of these sources, as there is no guarantee that every thesis is of high quality. And we shouldn't forget **popular scientific books**: books that are written by scholars, but in a more accessible style. In many cases, these books are also reliable, because their arguments are often backed up with references. You can usually include grey literature in your research bibliography (see also *Chapter 11*), but if you're not sure, you can ask your lecturer or supervisor whether the source you've found meets the requirements.

It is likely that one of the first things that you'll learn in academic circles is that Google and Wikipedia are unreliable: the former due to its commercial interests, the latter because anyone, in principle, can adjust the information and few checks are made on the content. But this doesn't mean that you are not permitted to use these tools. On Wikipedia, you will often find detailed overviews of scientific theories and findings. Although you may not cite these (see *Chapter 11* for more on citation rules), they sometimes contain useful citations or references to scientists and/ or publications associated with a theory or a method. Always use these sources as a means to another end: that of finding (and learning to understand) academic publications.

> ### TIP
> *You can use search operators to filter your Google search results. For example, it is possible to limit your results to PDF files by adding 'filetype: pdf' in the search bar. Useful overviews of search operators are available online (for more on search methods, see Box 1.1 on page 23).*

Scholarly search engines

A huge amount of scholarly research is published. To give you an idea: in the exact sciences, in 2015 alone there were more than 25,000 different peer-reviewed journals (a number that is growing by around 3% a year), and the popular scientific database Web of Science contains more than 40 million individual scientific sources. One of the greatest challenges for students, especially interdisciplinary students, is how to find the right needles in this vast haystack of scientific information. How can this be done? And what tools are available to help you?

Availability

A lot of information about academic sources can be found on the Internet, and almost all journals publish their articles online. In the case of most scholarly journals, you need to subscribe in order to get access (with the exception of *open access journals*, which provide content free of charge). When you're at university, you can make use of your institution's subscriptions; universities usually subscribe to thousands of journals. However, you will sometimes come across articles that cannot be accessed at your institution. If this happens, keep searching using standard search engines. For example, you may have the good fortune that the author has put the article online themselves. In that case, you could always email the author to ask for the article (authors don't receive royalties for articles, so they won't lose out if you don't buy it), or search for a different article instead.

The library

One source of knowledge that now seems rather old-fashioned is the physical library, such as the libraries run by educational institutions and municipalities. It is usually possible to search the collections using a digital search engine on the library's website. You might be tempted to ignore the dusty old library building and consult the digital library from your armchair, but in certain circumstances, this can be unwise. Books can be valuable, because they give authors the space to expand and describe ideas or research fields in all their complexity. As a result, a book will sometimes contain all the information you need in one fell swoop. And you will sometimes find a level of depth in a book that you'd never encounter in a scholarly article, because articles usually need to follow a tight structure. In *Chapter 2*, we will focus in more depth on the relationship between books and articles.

By now, most journals have digitized their older publications, but this is not always the case. During your Internet search, you may therefore be referred to the library, where you can pick up a hard copy of the article or have it sent to you. Most educational institutions have an efficient system that allows you to call up paper journals rapidly or have them delivered to your faculty.

Digital search engines and databases

Various **databases** and **search engines** can be used to search scholarly journals. Most of them contain many thousands of journals, and sometimes millions of individual scientific sources.

Students and researchers mainly use these search engines to search for relevant scholarly literature for their research. Perhaps the best known is Google Scholar, which is popular among students – partly due to familiarity with the brand. However, it is not the only search engine (nor is it necessarily the best). Through your university, you may also have access to other disciplinary and interdisciplinary search machines with extensive search functions for specialized databases, such as the Web of Science, Pubmed, Science Direct, and Scopus.

Search methods

All of these search engines allow you to search for scholarly sources in different ways. You can search by topic, author, year of publication, and journal name. Some tips for **searching for literature**:

1. Use a combination of search terms that accurately describes your topic.
2. You should use mainly English search terms, given that English is the main language of communication in academia.
3. Try multiple search terms to unearth the sources you need.
   a. Ensure that you know a number of synonyms for your main topic
   b. Use the search engine's thesaurus function (if available) to map out related concepts.

If you want to do research into financial crises, for example, search for 'falling property prices', 'banking crisis', 'decline in economic performance', or a combination of these. The ideal combination of search terms is different for each topic: overly general keywords can result in too many search results, overly specific keywords can produce too few. You should therefore use operators and commands to refine your search combinations. You will find several useful operators and commands in *Box 1.1*.

> **TIP**
>
> *During your search, it is advisable to keep track of the keywords and search combinations you use. This will allow you to check for blind spots in your search strategy, and you can get feedback on improving the search combinations. Some search engines automatically keep a record of this. What's more, if you're writing a review paper or literature review, for example, you can describe your search functions in your methods section.*

Box 1.1   Operators and commands for search engines (adapted from Sanders, 2011)

Command	Explanation	Example
AND	Search only for terms that occur together.	desertification AND carbon dioxide
OR	Search for articles containing one of the two terms.	acidification OR acidified
NOT	Do not include this term.	sustainability NOT pollution
*	Variation on words.	econ* (gives results for economy, economical, economic, etc.)
" "	Search for this exact phrase.	"social unrest in Ukraine"
~	Search for synonyms.	~cognition (also gives results for: apprehension, awareness, intelligence, perception, etc.)

Ordering your search results

In the digital library, it is often possible to order your search results in different ways. For example, you can rank the articles according to the *date of publication*, with the most or least recent article at the top. Although this is important (studies can date), it does not immediately help you with your initial search. You can also rank them according to *relevance*; in that case, the articles at the top of the list are those closest to your search terms. Early on in your research, though, it is most useful to rank your results on the basis of *references*. In this case, the articles at the top of the list are those that are used most often by other authors and best reflect the key debates and research in the field you've identified. Later, when you start to read more thoroughly and search for new texts based on this (see *Chapter 2*), you'll find it more useful to rank articles on the basis of relevance or date.

Continuous search

Searching for literature is a dynamic process. It won't be enough simply to read your first ten search results; you need to keep ordering and assessing the literature you've found, and keep searching for different and/or better search results and more relevant articles. One tip for guiding this dynamic process is to use your search results to find more relevant sources.

First, articles often give an overview of the **keywords** that are relevant to this article (listed after the abstract), and you can use these keywords to help you to refine or improve your search combination. Second, search engines such as Google Scholar often give you the option of searching the other way round; that is, looking at which recent articles refer to a particular article that you've already found. To do this, click on the 'cited by' link in the search result. This allows you to find more recent sources that build on the information in the source you've found (see *Figure 1.2*). This is also a useful way to get an overview of the scholarly debate surrounding a particular theme.

What's more, search engines often give you the option of searching for 'related articles', and these literature suggestions can also help you when searching for other relevant sources. After downloading an article, some search engines automatically open a pop-up window suggesting similar articles. Don't close this window out of hand, as it will often contain useful suggestions. You can also ask the search engine to notify you when certain publications in your field of interest are published.

Figure 1.2 A scholarly article is embedded in the literature

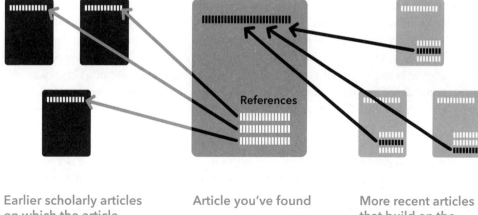

Earlier scholarly articles on which the article you've found builds

Article you've found

More recent articles that build on the article you've found

Exploratory reading

Now that you're familiar with the wonderful world of academia and have a general sense of what your research will be about, you need to make a start on your actual research. How do you make a selection from the enormous number of articles that are often available on a topic? Keep the following four questions in mind, and use them to guide your literature review:

- What is already known about my topic and in which discipline is the topic discussed?
- Which theories and concepts are used and discussed within the scope of my topic, and how are they defined?
- How is my topic researched and what different research methods are there?
- Which questions remain unanswered and what has yet to be researched?

These questions will remain important throughout the exploratory phase. In the final section of this chapter, we describe a reading technique that allows you to filter large chunks of text rapidly, so you can gauge whether it is relevant for your research. In *chapters 2 and 3*, we describe additional reading techniques that allow you to delve more deeply into a text.

Speed reading

In order to guide the **speed reading** technique, you can use theories and concepts (as discussed above). When speed reading, you familiarize yourself rapidly with a text and consider how it relates to the other texts you've found. The following components are present in most articles, and they will help you to extract the key theories and concepts from the article.

First of all, an article or a book chapter has a *title*. The title is often a condensed summary of the whole publication, reduced to a single sentence. Given that most research involves trying to find a relationship (theory) between concepts, you can be pretty sure that the title will contain one or more concepts. The *title of the book or journal* can also be a good indication. Not only do titles often contain concepts and theories, but they also indicate the disciplinary or interdisciplinary field in which the text is located. What's more, nearly all articles include an *abstract*. This is a brief summary of the whole study; not only the results, but also the approach and the theoretical basis. The abstract is often followed by several keywords, which often include concepts, too.

Run through the titles, abstracts, and keywords of the articles at the top of your list and work out which ideas (concepts) keep coming back. Next, use the abstract to figure out what these concepts mean, and also try to see whether they are connected and whether this differs for each study. If you are unable to work out what the concepts mean, based on the context, don't hesitate to use dictionaries or search engines. Make a list of the concepts that occur most frequently in these texts, and try to draw links between them. A good way to do this is to use a **concept map**, which sets out the links between the concepts in a visual way; see *Figure 1.3*.

Figure 1.3 This concept map is based on the introduction to the research article in Appendix B. The theoretical framework used to explain the concepts and the relationships between them has been represented visually. The different possibilities in the model are shown in red and green. Obviously, you can put what you like here, depending on your aim. If you want to know which relationships have already been researched and which have not, for example, you could expand the concept map by adding references to articles you've read. If your aim is to understand the text thoroughly, you could devise and add your own examples, as has been done in the orange blocks..

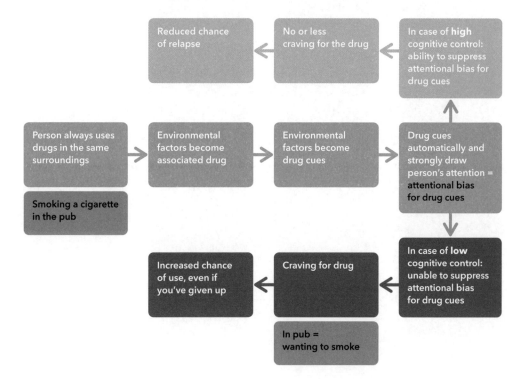

All being well, by now you will have found a list of articles and used them to identify several concepts and theories. From these, try to select the theories and concepts that you want to explore further. This choice isn't set in stone, of course; you can broaden your search again later if you fail to find a good research question based on the current selection. However, selecting at this stage will help you to frame and focus your research.

The next step is to discover to what extent these articles deal with these concepts and theories in similar or different ways, and how combining these concepts and theories leads to different outcomes. In order to do this, you will need to read more thoroughly and make a detailed record of what you've learned; and that is what we shall focus on in the next chapter.

Sources

Menken, S., & Keestra, M. (eds.). (2016). *An introduction to interdisciplinary research: Theory and practice.* Amsterdam: Amsterdam University Press.

Sanders, E. (2011). *Eerste hulp bij e-onderzoek voor studenten in de geesteswetenschappen: Slimmer zoeken, slimmer documenteren.* Retrieved from https://openaccess.leidenuniv.nl/handle/1887/17774

Vigen, T. (n.d.). *Spurious correlations.* Retrieved from http://tylervigen.com/spurious-correlations

Walliman, N. (2011). *Research methods: The basics.* USA: Routledge.

Other useful sources

Useful popular-science journals for finding a topic include:

- *New Scientist*: www.newscientist.com
- *Scientific American*: www.scientificamerican.com
- IFLScience: www.iflscience.com

For more practical tips on how to study successfully, go to www.uva.nl/en/home and type 'study skills' into the page's search function, and then go to 'studying successfully'. The tip sheet 'How do you read smartly' is particularly useful for the various reading strategies.

2 Gathering and organizing key information

A second academic skill that is used in the preparatory phase of research is being able to distinguish effectively between core and supporting information in a text. This is an important skill to have, whether you're preparing for a research project or revising for an exam. How can you make sense of the overwhelming quantity of information to be found in books, articles, seminars, and lectures, and how do you extract the information that is relevant?

First of all, it is important to create an optimal learning environment, so you can use your time as efficiently as possible to get to the heart of a text. What's more, it is important to know which *learning objective* you're working towards, so you know what kind of information you need to save. Finally, various *reading strategies* can help you extract essential information from a wide range of texts.

Optimizing your study environment

Perhaps the grades for my recent exams are already online? As you're reading a text, you'll notice that it's hard to stop thoughts such as these popping into your mind. Lots of students are familiar with this problem: whether the distraction is an upcoming grade or social media, your studies are interrupted and your results suffer as a consequence.

Many people find it helpful to study in blocks of 25-45 minutes, taking short breaks in between. During these blocks, you should not allow yourself to be distracted by outside stimuli or your own thoughts. This method is known as the **pomodoro technique** (named after its Italian inventor, who used a tomato-shaped kitchen timer to measure out 25-minute blocks), and it's a great one to try if you are having trouble concentrating. See 'Other useful sources' at the end of this chapter for a website that explains the pomodoro technique in more detail.

In order to improve your concentration, it is important to **limit distractions while you're studying** (see *Box 2.1*) Turn off your phone, make sure that your email program is closed if you are working at your computer, and don't allow yourself to visit social media or news sites. If you need to study on your laptop (when writing a research paper, for example), there are all kinds of useful apps that can temporarily block social media; see 'Other useful sources' for an overview.

Box 2.1   *Distractions while studying*

What many students think:	What research shows:
My telephone doesn't distract me at all - in fact, it helps me to study.	Negative effect of telephones on cognitive learning during lectures (Wei, Wang & Klausner, 2012).
If I use my laptop, I take much better notes.	Making notes on a laptop leads to less learning than making notes on paper (Mueller & Oppenheimer, 2014).
If I read the literature on my laptop, I remember much more.	Students can give better answers to questions about a printed text than about a digital text they have read online (Mangen, Walgermo & Brønnick, 2013).

Not everyone learns in the same way and not everyone is distracted by the same things. Ask yourself the following questions to find out which method of concentration works best for you: for how long can you concentrate at a time? At which time of day are you at your best: for example, are you a morning person or an evening person? What do you find difficult (writing an essay, for example)? Where do you study best: at home or in the library? What is most time-consuming: reading literature or writing papers? Depending on the answers, you can choose the concentration method that suits you best.

Learning objectives

You often read a text because you want to learn something or find something out. When you read a text, you focus on finding the information that is stored there. You might also be interested in understanding the author's argument, or in assessing the correctness of their arguments or theories. The objective that you set yourself when reading a text influences how you prepare for reading, your reading speed, and whether (and how) you take notes. Before you start reading, it is important to ask yourself the following questions:

- In how much detail do I want to understand this text?
- How much prior knowledge do I have on this topic?
- How much do I want to remember of this text after I've read it?
- Do I need to criticize this text?
- Is it important to draw links between this text and the lectures or other sources?

How you answer these questions will determine how you can best approach the text. You will have noticed that it is not always necessary to read a text from left to right and from beginning to end, as you would a novel, for example. In some cases, you are expected to ask yourself these questions and figure out what's needed for the assignment. In most cases, though, the assignment will set a number of **learning objectives**. Learning objectives are the theme that runs through every course, and they are often used to link an assignment with an overarching learning task. In many educational institutions, lecturers are taught to link learning objectives as effectively as possible to all of the components of a course: lectures, exams, assignments, and assessments.

It should come as no surprise, then, that learning objectives enjoy such a prominent place in course handbooks, lectures, and seminars. As a student, do make use of this; if you know what the learning objective is, you will know how detailed your knowledge-gathering needs to be. When doing an **exam** or submitting an assignment, this can make the difference between passing and failing. There is a difference, for example, between being able to reproduce the figures and concepts that you come across in a lecture or text, and being able to apply these concepts in new contexts.

Depending on the learning objective, you will need to study the course material at different levels. Sometimes lecturers will give you practice questions, but if they don't, the learning objectives should give you an insight into this. Learning objectives are often based on **Bloom's classification**, which divides objectives into different levels of knowledge: remembering, understanding, applying, analysing, and evaluating (Bloom et al., 1956). Sometimes, you just need to reproduce knowledge ('remembering') and explain it in your own words ('understanding'), something that is often required in exams. Other times, there are essay questions that require you to apply theories or concepts to new cases ('applying'), interpret particular research data ('analysing'), or even give your own critical assessment ('evaluating'). All being well, the course handbook will explain how the learning objectives are linked to the exams.

Reading strategies

When reading texts, it is best to take detailed notes and distinguish *major* issues from *minor* ones. When doing this, it is important to distinguish between the sources of knowledge that you use: are you going to read textbooks, academic books, or articles?

Reading textbooks

You will encounter different types of books in the academic world. Some books are written by scholars to provide an overview of their field; these books can be read in a similar way to academic articles (see below). Then there are more theoretical and philosophical books, which are written by authors in order to develop ideas. These texts are sometimes difficult and complex; we shall spend more time on them in *Chapter 3*. And then there are textbooks that have been produced specially for a certain discipline. Often very accessible, these books are a good place to start when learning how to get to the heart of a text quickly.

Textbooks often work with concepts, as well as various theories that define these concepts in a number of different ways (see *Chapter 1*). The great thing about these books is that they frequently highlight concepts or put them in bold or different colours, making them easy to spot – and thus making it very easy to make notes. It's a question of reading through the highlighted concepts and underlining the accompanying explanations. It is wise to underline just the amount of text that allows you to understand the concept and how it is used; don't underline more than this, as it reduces the utility of making notes.

It is also a good idea to make connections between concepts as you are reading textbooks. One way to visualize the relationships between concepts is to make a concept map, in which you sketch out the links between the concepts and theories (see *Chapter 1*). Finally, assuming it's your own copy, don't hesitate to jot down your own thoughts in the margin: what something reminds you of, where you read something like this before, and, above all, how this relates to other concepts in the text.

> **TIP**
>
> At the end of each chapter, it is a good idea to rewrite or retype all of the concepts and their definitions, so that you have one overarching list of concepts. Before an exam, you can compare this list with the content of the lectures, learning objectives, and mock exam questions.

Reading academic articles and books

Making notes on academic articles and books is slightly more complicated. Academic publications can take a number of forms, the most important ones being articles, review articles, and books. **Articles** (also known as 'research papers') are written with the aim of sharing academic work with a wider academic audience, and they often discuss empirical research. **Review articles** (also known as 'literature reviews') are overview studies that describe the key state-of-the-art findings in a discipline, or in a research field within a discipline.

In **academic books**, the state of the research in a whole research field is often mapped out. Sometimes these are overview studies consisting of work by multiple authors, and sometimes they are overview studies of a period in the work of one author. In general, they integrate or collect a lot of research and many literature reports.

In practice, as a young researcher, you will tend to use academic articles; and because these have a fixed structure (and the structure of books and review articles can differ somewhat), we have chosen to focus on academic articles here. The structure used by these articles is often determined more by the research they are exploring than ease of reading. Although the structure can differ slightly from the norm at the level of detail, most articles consist of an introduction, a middle section, and a discussion (the IMD structure; see also *Chapter 9* on how this structure works).

If you only need to extract essential information from a text for an exam or your own research, you certainly don't need to read all of the sections. The *introduction* and the *conclusion* are often good starting points for quickly discovering: 1) the central concepts and theories; 2) how they are operationalized (that is, how they are used in the research; see also *Part 2*); and 3) which research results this led to. It is often useful to scan the *methods* section to find out exactly what the researchers did with the above-mentioned concepts and theories. This section is often very technical, however, and laden with jargon that applies specifically to the researcher's field. If you only need to understand the essence of the text, you'll rarely need this level of detail.

As you would expect, the *results* section contains lots of relevant information. In quantitative studies, it is often the case that these results are expressed in highly technical jargon, too. Later in your course, you will do methodological modules that explain this jargon. In the early stages of your course, the main thing is to understand the interpretation of the results that is given. You should thus look carefully at what the author has made of the data shown. In doing so, focus particularly on the *figures*, which reiterate the main message. What do they say, and how is this interpreted?

Systematic reading

Not only is it important to understand the structure of the text and know which sections you need to focus on, but it is also important to know how you should then extract key information from the text. You can do this by using the technique known as **systematic reading**. For this, it can be helpful to distinguish the line of argument. A line of argument is made up of *central positions*, which themselves consist of arguments with accompanying explanations and/or examples. Sometimes these positions are easy to recognize from statements such as: 'In this study, it will be argued that...'

Sometimes, however, the arguments are less easy to recognize – but the good news is that here, too, it can be really helpful to identify **concepts** and **theories**. As these are the building blocks of scholarly research, it is almost impossible to introduce a line of argument in a paper without using any concepts or theories. Other components that allow you to recognize the line of argument include *enumerations* ('First, second' – see *Chapter 3* for more signal words). In some cases, the author will also make a *recommendation* in the line of argument on what should be done or where further research is needed. If you mark these things in your text, you will get a clearer idea of the central position and, with this, the essence of the text (see *Figure 2.1*).

Finally, it can be useful to take a closer look at the *figures* and *images*. What do they say? How are they used in the text? Are they used illustratively or do they show a research result?

Figure 2.1 *Example of a text that has been marked up using the systematic reading technique*
Source of the original text: Bierman (2014)

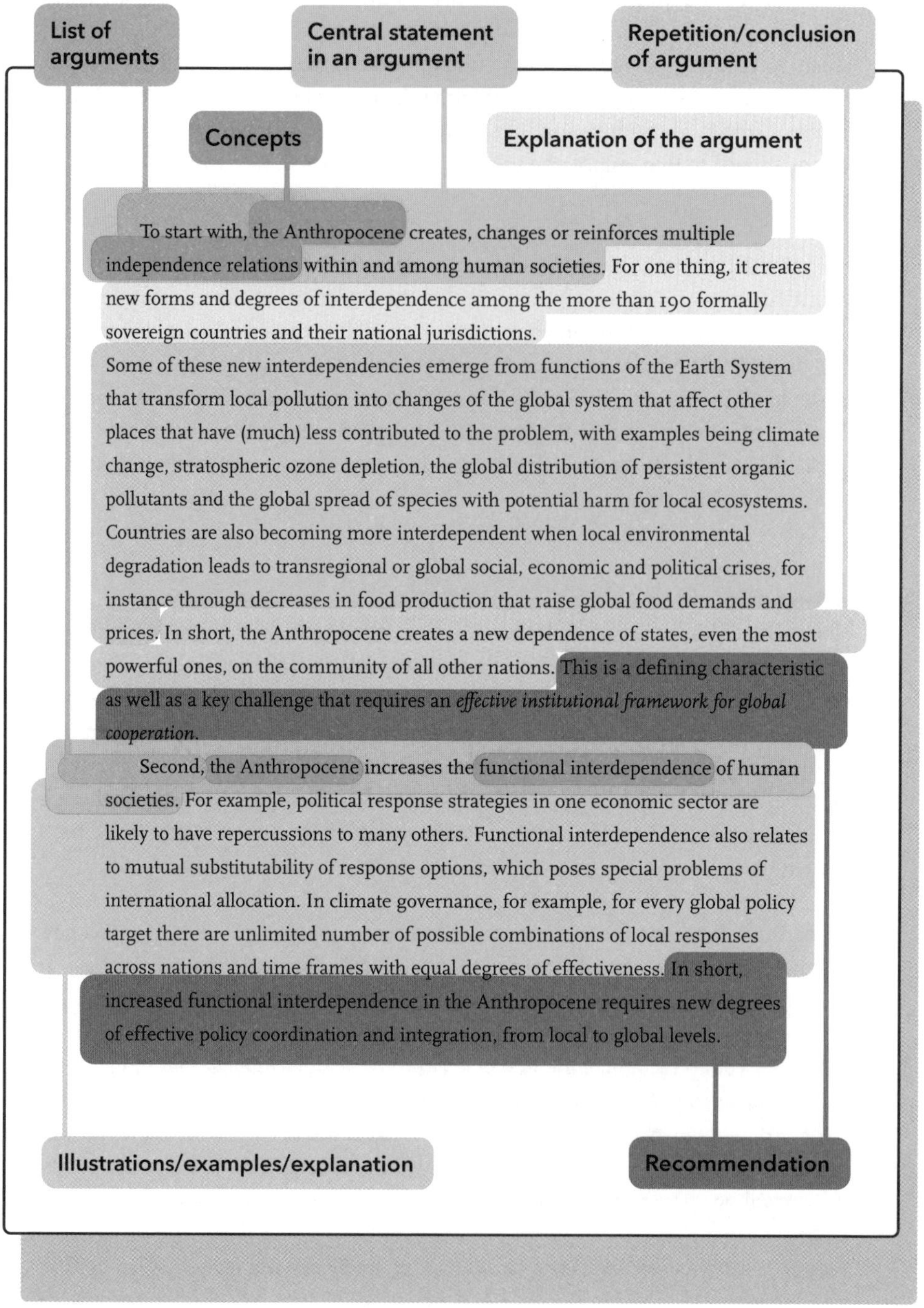

List of arguments

Central statement in an argument

Repetition/conclusion of argument

Concepts

Explanation of the argument

To start with, the Anthropocene creates, changes or reinforces multiple independence relations within and among human societies. For one thing, it creates new forms and degrees of interdependence among the more than 190 formally sovereign countries and their national jurisdictions. Some of these new interdependencies emerge from functions of the Earth System that transform local pollution into changes of the global system that affect other places that have (much) less contributed to the problem, with examples being climate change, stratospheric ozone depletion, the global distribution of persistent organic pollutants and the global spread of species with potential harm for local ecosystems. Countries are also becoming more interdependent when local environmental degradation leads to transregional or global social, economic and political crises, for instance through decreases in food production that raise global food demands and prices. In short, the Anthropocene creates a new dependence of states, even the most powerful ones, on the community of all other nations. This is a defining characteristic as well as a key challenge that requires an *effective institutional framework for global cooperation.*

Second, the Anthropocene increases the functional interdependence of human societies. For example, political response strategies in one economic sector are likely to have repercussions to many others. Functional interdependence also relates to mutual substitutability of response options, which poses special problems of international allocation. In climate governance, for example, for every global policy target there are unlimited number of possible combinations of local responses across nations and time frames with equal degrees of effectiveness. In short, increased functional interdependence in the Anthropocene requires new degrees of effective policy coordination and integration, from local to global levels.

Illustrations/examples/explanation

Recommendation

Organizing information

As you do your literature review, you will find and read many sources. So many, in fact, that after some time you will no longer know which sources you've already read and which information is relevant. If you are reading texts in order to write an article, it is essential to keep track of the sources you've found and what kind of information you have got (or can get) from them. You should start doing this as you scan the search results. When you study your sources thoroughly and critically, it is important to make a personal record of which information is relevant for further research. If you are using **reference management software** (see *Chapter 11*), it is a good idea to save important articles directly in your software program.

This process can be streamlined by using a so-called **literature matrix**: an overview in a spreadsheet (in Microsoft Excel, for example, or in a table in Microsoft Word) where you save all of the relevant information that you find for each concept. Always include the page number where you found the information. You can also cut and paste sentences from articles that are (or might be) important for your research. This may help you to avoid plagiarism later, because it allows you to distinguish between the original wording and your own phrasing (see also *Chapter 12*). Add a few sentences to the overview on why you think the source is usable, and why the concept is useful within the overarching theme of your topic. In this way, you not only gather sources, but you also organize them.

For example, suppose that you want to do research for your exploratory study into the relationship between meat and environmental damage. It might have struck you that 'water use' is a common concept used by the most frequently cited authors. *Table 2.1* can then be used to keep track of different opinions on the definition of 'water use'.

Box 2.2   Example of a literature matrix (adapted from De Jong, 2011)

Concepts	Text 1 (Author, Year, Definition)	Text 2 (Author, Year, Definition)	Text 3 (Author, Year, Definition)	Notes
Water use	Baroni et al. (2007) define water use as the percentage of total fresh water consumption that is taken up by production (p. 285)	Ercin et al. (2012) describe water use as the total volume of fresh water that is used indirectly or directly for a product (p.392)	Renault and Wallender (2000) do not define water use as such, but 'water productivity': the ratio of the mass of the product versus the water consumed' (p.277)	The definition used by Baroni et al. (2007) is not specific enough (for example)
Meat production				
Land use				

The first articles you find and select may not contain all the information you are looking for. This can be a recurring problem in your research study, certainly in the early stages, but don't let this discourage you. Instead, use the literature matrix to identify the remaining gaps.

Sources

Bierman, F. (2014). The Anthropocene: A governance perspective. *The Anthropocene Review, 1*(1), 57-61.

Bloom, B.S., Englehart, M.D., Furst, E.J., Hill, W.H., & Krathwohl, D.R. (1956). *The Taxonomy of educational objectives, handbook I: The Cognitive domain.* New York: David McKay Company.

Flick, U. (2011). *Introducing research methodology: A beginner's guide to doing a research project.* London: Sage.

Jong, J. de (2011). *Handboek academisch schrijven: In stappen naar een essay, paper of scriptie.* Bussum: Uitgeverij Coutinho.

Mangen, A., Walgermo, B.R., & Brønnick, K. (2013). Reading linear texts on paper versus computer screen: Effects on reading comprehension. *International Journal of Educational Research, 58*, 61-68.

Mueller, P.A., & Oppenheimer, D.M. (2014). The pen is mightier than the keyboard: Advantages of longhand over laptop note taking. *Psychological Science, 25*(6), 1159-1168.

Wei, F.F., Wang, Y.K., & Klausner, M. (2012). Rethinking college students' self-regulation and sustained attention: Does text messaging during class influence cognitive learning? *Communication Edition, 61*(3), 185-204.

Other useful sources

You'll find many tools online that help you to maintain your concentration or plan efficiently. Here are some examples:

- The Forest app: this app for aiding concentration can be installed on your mobile phone. https://www.forestapp.cc/en/
- Ommwriter: if you find it difficult to start writing, Ommwriter creates a peaceful, distraction-free writing environment on your computer. https://ommwriter.com/
- Coffitivity: this website features a range of sound clips of background noise – useful if you're sitting in a packed library and are distracted by typing and coughing. https://coffitivity.com/
- Anti-social: this app blocks all social media on your computer for as long as you need to work. https://antisocial.80pct.com
- The Kanbanflow is a workflow planning website that offers an online environment for working with the pomodoro-timer technique. https://kanbanflow.com/
- Wunderlist is a program for your computer and telephone where you can save and organize all your to-do lists. https://www.wunderlist.com/
- The most dangerous writing app: this app punishes you if you stop writing for too long, by deleting all of your recent progress. http://www.themostdangerouswritingapp.com/

3 Studying thoroughly and critically

When you're getting to grips with a text, it can help to make the argument explicit. You can represent the structure of the argument in diagrammatical form, for example, or – if you're working with a difficult text – analyse the text at sentence level. In this chapter, we explain a method that you can use to understand a complex text. We also describe different forms of argumentation, which can help you when criticizing scholarly texts.

Sentence-level analysis

Techniques such as speed reading (see *Chapter 1*) and systematic reading (see *Chapter 2*) can often get you a long way, whether you're revising for an exam or trying to get a quick overview of a research field. Some theoretical and/or philosophical texts are more complicated, though, not least because they analyse and explain issues at a highly abstract level. If the theories themselves are difficult to understand or the line of argument is not immediately clear, it can be useful to approach the text as you would a text in a foreign language – when you need to analyse the text at sentence level before you can understand its core message.

In this case, too, it can be useful to identify concepts and theories, but not immediately. First, divide complicated sentences into several *main and subordinate clauses*. You can do this by looking at the conjunctions; the words that link the different sentences and sentence constituents. It can also be useful to look at whether these conjunctions are *coordinating* or *subordinate conjunctions*. If they are coordinating conjunctions (for example, 'and', 'but', 'or', 'then', 'thus', 'because'), you know that the two clauses are on a par and likely to be of equal importance. If subordinate conjunctions are used (for example, 'when', 'if', 'whilst', 'as soon as', 'before', 'for', 'now', 'then', 'after'), you know that a principal clause is being linked to a dependent clause. This helps you to understand the structure.

If a principal clause is followed by a dependent clause, this often means that the dependent clause further explains or develops the information given in the principal clause. Thus, when a writer states a view, they often do so in the principal clause, after which they explain their view in the dependent clause. Subsequently, for each principal and dependent clause, you can subdivide the text into *finite forms, subjects*, and *direct objects*.

As you're trying to understand a tricky text, it is useful to take note of the signs that the author has provided. Authors use connecting phrases and **signal words** to clarify the connections between sentences. This can be helpful when you are trying to figure out the relationship between arguments or data (see *Box 3.1* for possible signal words and their function within the structure of the sentence).

Box 3.1   *Signal words*

Structural function	Possible words
Enumeration	and, moreover, first, second, furthermore, what is more, not only, but also
Reason, cause, result	since, because, for the reason that, in order to, therefore
Condition	if, when, provided that, unless, when
Concession	although, admittedly, still
Contrast	however, on the other hand, in contrast, nevertheless, despite, on the one hand, still, while
Comparison	as if, as well as, also, equally, like, similarly
Summary	in short, in sum, to summarize
Conclusion	hence, it follows that, in conclusion it can be stated that
Degree of probability	probable, improbable, under normal circumstances, (un)likely

All of the above might seem like something out of secondary school, but it can be really helpful when trying to understand a complex text. Looking at which object or person forms the central focus, which verbs are linked to them, and which other objects and people are connected to these in turn, offers a rapid insight into the structure of a sentence. You can do this easily with a pen, using different shapes (circles, squares, triangles) to represent the different concepts, their relations, signal words and reference words (see *Figure 3.1*). And once you have understood the whole sentence, it is easier to understand the meaning of the concepts and theories.

Fear not; you won't need to use this method for the rest of your academic career. At a certain point, you'll understand the jargon and improve your reading technique, and you'll no longer need all of these extra aids. Until then, though, it can be helpful to keep using this method.

Figure 3.1   Example of a text that has been analysed at sentence level
Source of the original text: Madison, J. (1788). Article 10. The Federalist papers

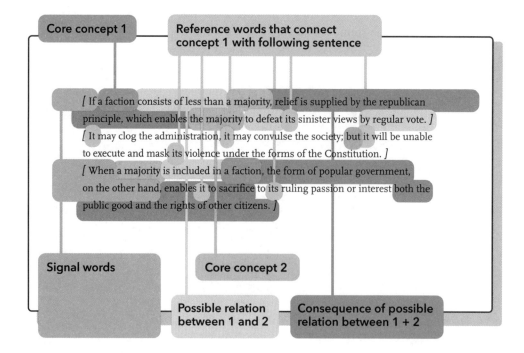

Types of argumentation

Sometimes, it's not enough to analyse the text at sentence level: although you may understand exactly what is being said, you may still be unsure about the precise point that the writer wants to make. In this case, one solution is to analyse the text at the **level of the argument** By identifying different types of argumentation and representing them in a handy, clear diagram, you can figure out the author's intentions more effectively. What's more, this gives you the option of critiquing the author's argument. We do this by drawing on a few examples from the literature review in *Appendix A*.

Simple argumentation

The most basic form of substantiation is the **simple argument**. With this, you defend a view using just one argument. In the example below, the argument that a vegetarian diet is healthier is used to convince the reader of the view that people should not eat meat:

People should not eat meat, because a vegetarian diet is healthier.

Simple argumentation

Plural argumentation

If you are defending a view, you will normally need to provide more than one argument. Putting forward a number of arguments strengthens a view, because even if one argument is disproved, the other arguments will continue to support the view. In the literature review, for example, two arguments are given for the view that people should not eat meat:

People should not eat meat because a vegetarian diet is healthier, and because not eating meat is better for the environment.

In this case, each individual argument supports the view; the arguments are self-standing. In principle, one argument would have sufficed. You can thus see **plural argumentation** as a combination of a number of single arguments that support the same view. We can represent this type of reasoning as follows:

Plural argumentation

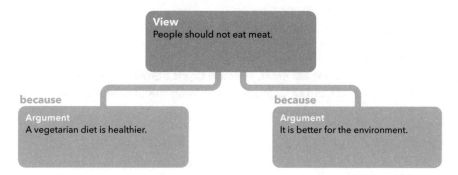

Coordinating argumentation

In other cases, the arguments supplied to support a view are used in such a way that they are inseparable:

The government's environmental policy is erratic. On the one hand, the government is supporting wind energy projects, while on the other hand, it is cutting back on subsidies for solar energy.

It is only possible to claim that the government's environmental policy is erratic if both of these opposing arguments hold. When arguments are intertwined in this way, we call this **coordinating argumentation**. One disadvantage of this argumentation is that if one argument falls, the case as a whole is undermined (in contrast to plural argumentation, for example). A coordinating argument can be represented diagrammatically as follows:

Coordinating argumentation

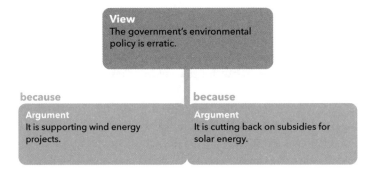

Subordinate argumentation

It is often necessary to substantiate an argument by using other arguments; for example, because you think the argument needs backing up in order to be credible:

People should not eat meat, because this is better for the environment. More water is needed to produce one kilogram of meat than to produce one kilogram of vegetables.

The view is that people should not eat meat, because this is better for the environment. In order to convince the reader that people really do need to cut down on the amount of meat they consume, the writer substantiates the argument that this is better for the environment with the argument that more water is needed to produce a kilogram of meat than a kilogram of vegetables. This latter argument is thus not a direct argument for the view, but supports the first argument (strengthening this argument, thereby strengthening the case as a whole). We call this **subordinate argumentation**. The structure of a subordinate argument is weaker than that of a plural argument. After all, if a single argument can be refuted, the whole line of argumentation falls. For example, if you could convincingly show that more water is not needed to produce meat than to produce vegetables, then the grounds for the argument above (that not eating meat is better for the environment) and ultimately the view itself (that people should not eat meat) would be undermined. This type of argument can be represented diagrammatically as follows:

Subordinate argumentation

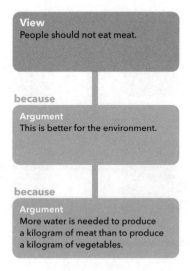

Now we know which forms of argumentation can be used, we can represent the structure of any text diagrammatically. You do this, first, by establishing what the writer's viewpoint is. Then you ask 'why?' and look for the answer in the text. With these arguments, you can again ask the 'why?' question, et cetera. Below you will find an example of an argument structure based on the article at the end of this book (*Appendix A*). If you are going to write your own texts, setting out the argumentation structure is a useful starting point for planning your article. We will return to this in *Chapter 9*.

Structure of argument derived from the sample paper in Appendix A

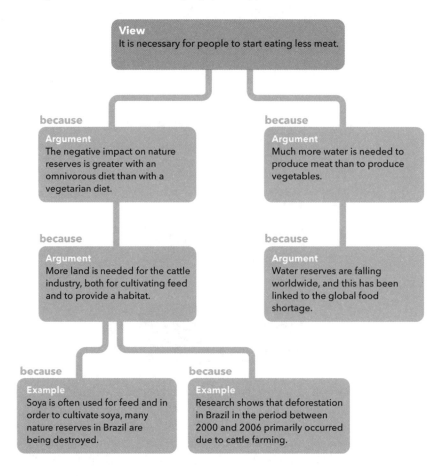

Implicit motivation

As shown above, argumentation consists of a viewpoint and (at least) an argument. But there is something else that is not reflected in the diagrams above: the relationship between the viewpoint and the argument. This is rarely stated explicitly, which is why it is also known as the **concealed argument**.

Take the argument: 'Elsa has mastered the material, she got ten out of ten.' Considering this argument critically, you could cast doubt on the point that's being made in two ways. First, you could cast doubt on the high grade: perhaps marking by a second examiner reveals that Elsa actually got a much lower grade. Suppose, though, that the test was marked a second time and Elsa did get ten out of ten; you could still criticize the argumentation by focusing on the relationship between the view and the argument. Is it really the case that getting a 'ten' proves that Elsa has a command of the material? Perhaps Elsa simply learned the answers to the questions by heart, and she is unable to apply the material to other cases.

The argument is thus based on a general assumption: 'If someone gets ten out of ten, they have a command of the material'. When analysing a text, it is wise to reflect on **implicit assumptions** such as these. Has the writer jumped to conclusions? These relationships between the viewpoint and the argument are not only helpful when critiquing a text, but also when elucidating the assumptions that are made by researchers (in a particular field). These assumptions can prove fertile ground for integrating different perspectives (see Menken & Keestra, 2016; see also 'reflecting on assumptions' in *Chapter 13*.

Critically evaluating texts

Now that you have learned to analyse a text at sentence level and assess the strength of its arguments using an argumentation diagram, you have taken the first steps towards critically evaluating a text. Nevertheless, it is important to look not only at what the text says, but also at the context in which it was written. You need to check the origins of all the sources you consult. Just because something is being claimed in a scholarly journal, this does not mean that it is incontrovertible (see also the fallacies in Chapter 9).

It is tempting, for example, to write something like, 'Author A (year) says this and THEREFORE it is true', in a literature review. However, this is not a good reflection of what academic research is. If you read an academic research report carefully, you'll see that the researchers qualify their claims and conclusions and put them in a particular context. Moreover, the **quality** of academic research varies; although much research is carried out meticulously, other studies are badly thought-out or incomplete. Therefore, in addition to finding relevant literature, it is also important to be able to analyse and discuss the quality of the research. *Box 3.2* contains a checklist for determining whether a particular article or journal is reliable.

By organizing, collecting and assessing theories, you will broaden your understanding of your research field – and this will ultimately allow you to sharpen the focus of your own research, too. The process of considering multiple theories provides a rapid insight into which issues have yet to be resolved in academia, and where there is still room for a new study or piece of research. This process of considering and discussing existing theories, accompanied by your own critical reflection on these and your own argument about where the theoretical gaps in scholarship lie, is also known as the **theoretical framework**. The process of weighing up theories and searching for as-yet-unexplored scientific fields will really help you to define your topic, and we will focus more on this in *Chapter 4*.

Box 3.2   Checklist: assessing the quality of academic literature

Criterion	What should you look at?	What should you watch out for?
Academic debate	Do the authors contextualize their findings more broadly? Do they mention limiting factors? Are these relevant for your research?	Not every academic medium answers these questions. Some of the grey literature, but also more popular scientific texts, focuses less on the broader implications of the research. That is not to say that this literature is unsuitable, but you should be extra critical.
Research design	Is it clear which choices have been made and why? Are other choices considered? Are the relevant steps taken in the research discussed?	Lack of experience may result in your being intimidated by jargon or statistical measurements, meaning that you tend to think: It must be OK. Nevertheless, even when you lack expertise, you can still say something meaningful about the choices that have been made and whether these have been substantiated.
Citations	Do other authors cite this article? Does the author have many citations from other authors?	A high citation score can also indicate controversial or weak research – something you should bear in mind. By contrast, if an article is not or hardly cited, this does not necessarily mean that the quality of the research isn't up to scratch. It may also mean that the research has yet to be picked up by the field, or that it has only just been published.
Journal impact factor	Does the journal have a high impact factor? (A journal's **impact factor** can be an indicator of its quality. You will find comprehensive lists of impact factors on the Internet.)	Again: scholarly journals with lower impact factors are not necessarily of inferior quality. They may also publish good research.

Sources

Baroni, L., Cenci, L., Tettamanti, M., & Berati, M. (2007). Evaluating the environmental impact of various dietary patterns combined with different food production systems. *European Journal of Clinical Nutrition, 61*(2), 279-286.

Ercin, A.E., Aldaya, M.M., & Hoekstra, A.Y. (2012). The water footprint of soy milk and soy burger and equivalent animal products. *Ecological Indicators, 18*, 392-402.

Madison, J. (1788). Article 10. *The Federalist papers*.

Menken, S. & Keestra, M. (eds.). (2016). *An Introduction to Interdisciplinary Research: Theory and Practice*. Amsterdam: Amsterdam University Press.

Renault, D., & Wallender, W.W. (2000). Nutritional water productivity and diets: From 'Crop per drop' towards 'Nutrition per drop'. *Agricultural Water Management, 45*, 275-296.

Other useful sources

The software package Rationale is a good option if you want to represent the structure of your argument diagrammatically. You can create a structure for free at rationaleonline.com. If you want to save or print out the argumentation structure, you will need to pay.

4 From your topic to your question

It can be very difficult to define how broad or narrow your topic can or should be in relation to the research project you're embarking upon. A 2,000-word literature review or a 10,000-word Master's thesis differ significantly in terms of the amount of depth you can achieve. Unfortunately, there is no golden rule for how long a project should be in relation to the chosen topic.

Concepts and theories can provide a good indication, however, as you can narrow or widen the scope by limiting or expanding the network of related concepts. In the literature review in *Appendix A*, for example, a single network of concepts (the relationships between meat production, soya production, soil use, and water use) is investigated. If you wanted to expand this research, you could broaden these concepts or choose to investigate several conflicting theories. In other words, defining your topic is a dynamic process. You start by mapping out the theories and concepts that you will need for your research question, but it is very likely that you will broaden or narrow these in the early stages.

Of course, it is important and really helpful to have an overview of all the relevant concepts and theories in the research field (or multiple fields, if you're doing interdisciplinary research) that sparked your interest. But having an overview is not sufficient to get you started on your own topic. First, because all of those theories and conceptualizations can contradict one another at times. It is the task of the researcher to take a clear position amongst the jumble of conflicting or complementary theories. This is often done in the **theoretical framework**.

Second, it is insufficient to have an understanding of the existing theory. You also need to identify the knowledge gaps in this overview, in order to discover which relationships between concepts have yet to be researched (or which methods have yet to be used to investigate these relationships). This is known as the **problem statement**: a statement of what, based on the theory, has yet to be clarified about the topic, and why it is essential to investigate this. Based on this statement, you will finally be able to formulate your **research question**: the question that will shape the rest of your research.

Theoretical framework

Theoretical frameworks can differ from study to study. This is because, first of all, theory is used in different ways in academic research. For example, there are disciplines that do not approach theory as it is conceived here, namely as theory in **empirical scholarship**: a relationship between concepts. For example, some theories are not descriptive, but prescriptive (also known as normative theory). In the field of ethics in philosophy, for example, we come across many ideas about how people should act in certain situations. In addition, theory can also mean the *history of ideas*. In this case, rather than using theories and concepts to explain reality, you use them to study the ideas that underlie these concepts. In political science, for example, one could write a theoretical framework on different concepts of liberty (negative versus positive) and how these have changed over the centuries (Maussen & Moret, 2014).

Aside from precisely which theoretical framework is used, studies can also differ in terms of the role the theoretical framework plays within them. For example, there are *purely methodological papers* in which the theoretical framework mainly indicates the state of existing research in a field. And *conceptual-theoretical studies* frequently omit the 'debate' between different theories, because this is already covered in the research. Often, the theoretical framework of these studies offers a general description of the theories that are addressed in detail later in the study.

In this book, we focus mainly on the role of theory in the *empirical cycle*. The theoretical framework plays a prominent role in this, because it not only outlines the state of the research field, but it also demarcates the niche where you, the researcher, are intending to contribute to knowledge in one or more research fields.

From theories to concepts and dimensions

In order to find that niche, you must look at what other researchers have done, first broadly and then in increasing detail. In practice, the reasoning is often the other way around. Especially in action research or transdisciplinary research (where you draw on knowledge from outside academia and you often work on specific cases), you start with a certain problem and come up with theories to explain it. Even then, however, you start with a broad theoretical basis, and you try to keep narrowing it down until you identify the aspects of a theory that is relevant to describing and/or explaining your case.

Based on your exploratory literature review, you built up a picture of the key authors and their most important articles. And in these articles, you were able to find the most common theories. These theories consist of concepts that, in turn, are defined in different ways. Take the literature review that is featured at the end of this book as an example. A literature review can be a piece of self-standing research (such as in *Appendix A*), but it can also be the first report in what will eventually become a research study. Based on the literature study, the broad topic of the environmental impact of eating meat is narrowed down to a comparison between eating soya and meat and the use of land and water. This is a well-defined topic for a literature review.

For a research study in which you want to generate your own results, though, the topic needs to be narrowed down further – primarily because you want to identify a **gap in the existing knowledge**, an aspect that has yet to be researched. However, this does not automatically mean that you need to produce new data or information in order to contribute to scholarship. Taking a new approach to the literature (such as in a literature review) or discussing it in a different context (a new case) are often excellent ways of doing scientifically relevant research, too. In these cases, you are also looking for gaps in the existing knowledge.

A good way to find a 'niche' in your chosen research field is to keep investigating which **dimensions** of the concepts are identified by the different authors. By this, we mean the 'scope' of the concept; what possible meanings are included in the concept by the author(s). Identifying the different dimensions helps you to define which aspects of the concept you want to measure and which you do not. In doing so, you can use a literature matrix like the one used in *Chapter 3*, but you can now expand or deepen it further

In the example (*Box 4.1*), there is a clear division between authors who look at the total use in production (water use) and those who take additional factors into account (water footprint). By looking in such detail, you will quickly spot the contrasts and similarities, but above all the gaps. For example, you could look in even more detail at the 'whole production chain', and at whether there are parts of the chain that have yet to be investigated in relation to water use and meat consumption. Or you could look at areas where the water-footprint method has been used, and whether there is a new dimension (for example, soya production) of another relevant concept that has yet to be included in existing research.

This whole process is covered in the theoretical framework: from the general description of the relationships between the concepts, and the more specific description of the differences in the dimensions identified by the authors, to the gap in the knowledge you think can be observed. When you eventually write this up, it is therefore important to follow a clear, strong line of argumentation; see *Chapter 9* of this book.

Box 4.1   Concepts and dimensions

Theory	Concepts	Dimensions	Application (source, empiricism, anecdotes)
Meat production, soya production, and water use	Water use (Baroni et al., 2007)	Water consumption for production	Water use: (water consumption) 70% of total fresh water by livestock and agriculture
	Water footprint (Ercin et al., 2012) = total volume of fresh water that is used directly or indirectly to produce a product	Direct water footprint (water consumed in the production of a certain product)	Water footprint (indirect and direct): water use of meat burger 14 x larger than that of a vegetarian burger
		Indirect water footprint (water consumption in whole production chain)	

The theoretical framework and interdisciplinary research

When you do interdisciplinary research, your theoretical framework is where you link several theoretical perspectives together; it is where you describe how different disciplines approach similar concepts differently.

Taking the example from *Box 4.1*, this could mean that a natural scientist and a humanities scholar take different approaches to water use. For example, there are humanities scholars who think about how water is represented. Whereas the concept of 'water use' may be conceived in the way defined in *Box 4.1*, as running water, it is also possible to define water at different points in the water cycle, such as the moment of precipitation, rather than the point at which it joins water flows that ultimately lead to consumption (Da Cunha, 2018). This is an example of how contrasting conceptualizations can lead to interdisciplinary integration (see also Menken & Keestra, 2016), for it invites a debate between humanities scholars and natural scientists about how water use should be defined and used in interdisciplinary research.

The problem statement

The theoretical framework ends with the establishment of the knowledge gap; in the **problem statement** you argue why this gap should be filled with your study. Two factors are important in this: scholarly and social relevance.

Scientific relevance means the value that your research will add to existing scientific practice. This relevance can be demonstrated in many ways. For example, this could concern the lack of data that your research is going to rectify, but it could also be about proving that a previous theory is wrong or qualifying an existing theory. Or, on the contrary, it could entail integrating two research fields (the holy grail of interdisciplinary research). You might also want to test a research result from one context in a new one (for example, a study that is set up in one country and carried out in another one, under different conditions).

Second, filling the knowledge gap must be **socially relevant**. This means that your research findings should be of interest to society in a broad sense, from businesses to NGOs, and from governments to fellow citizens. When making the case for social relevance, it is often useful to think of a particular target group and to try to put yourself in their shoes; or reflect on current social debates in the media or politics, and the extent to which this study could contribute to them.

Be aware that the problem statement can play different roles in different disciplines. In some disciplines, the problem statement is only mentioned in the introduction, after which it is explained further in the theoretical framework. In other disciplines, however, the problem statement follows on from the theoretical framework, and more or less forms the conclusion to this section – and thereby the bridge to your research question (see *Chapter 5*). There are also disciplines where the problem statement is synonymous with the entire research question and sub-questions, and sometimes the whole introduction. This means that you should always check the description of the assignment carefully to see what is meant by the 'problem statement'. Also be aware of how this differs from the **problem description** of **problem sketch** (which is often meant to be a broad introduction to the case that you're researching).

The problem statement provides the perfect overture to the phrasing of the research question. The theoretical framework explains what has and hasn't been researched yet, and in the problem statement, this is summarized as the research objective. The question should then be phrased in such a way that the research objective is captured as precisely as possible, in the form of the question that is answered at the end of the study. When you phrase this question, you're actually starting to define the structure of the rest of your study. We explain how to formulate a research question in *Chapter 5*.

Sources

Baroni, L., Cenci, L., Tettamanti, M., & Berati, M. (2007). Evaluating the environmental impact of various dietary patterns combined with different food production systems. *European Journal of Clinical Nutrition, 61*(2), 279-286.

Da Cunha, D. (2018). River literacy and the challenge of a rain terrain. In D. Venkat Rao (ed.), *Critical Humanities from India. Contexts, Issues, Futures*. India: Routledge.

Ercin, A.E., Aldaya, M.M., & Hoekstra, A.Y. (2012). The water footprint of soy milk and soy burger and equivalent animal products. *Ecological Indicators, 18*, 392-402.

Maussen, M., & Moret, M. (2014). *Academische vaardigheden voor politicologen*. Amsterdam: College voor Sociale Wetenschappen.

Menken, S., Keestra, M. (eds.). (2016). *An Introduction to Interdisciplinary Research*. Amsterdam: Amsterdam University Press.

5 Formulating a good question

Once you've decided which concepts and which dimension(s) of these concepts you're going to research, and you've reflected on the potential relationships between these concepts, it is time to capture this in a clear research question.

Characteristics of a research question

When it comes to academic problems, it's hardly ever the case that you formulate the perfect **research question** in one go. Drafting a good research question is one of the most difficult, but also one of the most important, aspects of academic research. It is an *iterative process* in which you go back and forth between the literature you've read and your research question, and you will probably draft many versions before coming up with the definitive one. A number of factors are important in this respect; see *Box 5.1*.

Box 5.1   *Checklist for research questions*

You do not always need to cover the following issues literally in your research question, but they should be clear from your argumentation and described in your introduction.

Relevance	Is the scholarly or social significance of the question clear? This shows why your question is worth researching. This is often clear from your problem statement.
Precision	Is the question formulated in an unambiguous way? State what you want to study as precisely as possible. This helps you to avoid answering the wrong question in your research. In other words, ensure that your question is sufficiently defined.
Feasibility	Can the question be answered? This means that the question must be formulated in such a way that it leads to a suitable research design. Ideally, you should be able to infer from the question how it should be answered.
Positioning within field	Is the question of sufficient scholarly quality? It is important to reflect on whether your question can be answered within a scholarly field. Check whether your topic fits within the area of knowledge you have in mind.

Types of questions

Academic questions can be divided into roughly two sorts of questions. First, you have **comparative questions**. These are questions whereby you compare two or more concepts, or look at the relationship between them. For example:

> *What are the differences between X and Y?*
>
> What are the differences between a vegetarian and an omnivorous diet?

> *What is the relationship between X and Y?*
>
> To what extent is there a relationship between water footprint and the quantity of meat consumed?

Another option is to compare the concept across two or more groups. For example:

> *To what extent is X different in group A than in group B?*
>
> What is the difference in the water footprint of a vegetarian and an omnivorous diet?

Finally, you can formulate a comparative question by contrasting the concept measured in your research with a certain criterion. Of course, this is only possible if generally applicable criteria exist. For example:

> *To what extent is X, as measured here, commensurable with the general criterion for X?*
>
> To what extent is the water footprint measured in the group of Dutch vegetarians commensurable with the water footprint of the average Dutch person?

Second, you have **explanatory questions**. With these, you try to unravel the explanations that underlie a phenomenon, something that is particularly common in literature reviews. An example of such a question is:

> *To what extent do X and/or Y explain Z?*
>
> To what extent can meat production and soya production explain the increase in the global water footprint?

Naturally, there are disciplines where other sorts of questions are used. In design studies, for example, we come across questions such as:

> *How can objective X be achieved?*

> How can the Dutch meat sector reduce its CO_2 emissions by 30% by 2030?

In this case, the answer is a description of the objective and an action plan setting out the steps that need to be taken in order to achieve this. Bear in mind that research questions such as these are only appropriate for studies that seek to develop a solution or scenario for a particular research problem.

Thus, when formulating your question, anticipate the type of answer that will follow. As you can see above, the structure of the answer can be inferred from the form of the question. If you reflect on this in advance, you will avoid a situation in which you're unable to answer your question with the resources to hand. The answer to your research question doesn't need to be definitive, though. For example, a literature review can end with a conclusion such as: 'There are two studies (Bergen, 2012; Smith, 2005) that make a reasonable case that... A third study by Janssen et al. (2014) nuances this by showing how...'

In addition, it is very important to **delimit** your question. In other words, the terms and concepts that make up the question should be defined as clearly and specifically as possible, so that it is clear exactly what you want to research. For example, it is very important to specify the concept that you are going to investigate in your question. A question such as: 'What influence does the agrarian sector have on the environment?' contains the concepts 'agrarian sector' and 'environment'. However, these concepts have a great many different dimensions; the agrarian sector, for example, covers crop cultivation, horticulture, livestock, and so on. The environment covers water quality, air quality, soil pollution, biodiversity, and so forth.

Try to formulate your question in such a way that the dimension you want to research is made clear, such as: 'To what extent does crop cultivation have an impact on water quality?' The final step is often to specify the location and/or the case. For example: 'To what extent does the cultivation of potatoes in Flevoland have an impact on eutrophication in this region?'

Another option is to specify these dimensions in sub-questions. In this case, you take a **main question** and divide it into **sub-questions**. For example, the main question could be: 'What influence does dairy farming have on greenhouse gas emissions?' You can subsequently divide the concept of greenhouse gas into different dimensions and answer each sub-question. For example:
1 'What influence does dairy farming have on methane gas emissions?'
2 'What influence does dairy farming have on carbon dioxide emissions?'

You then address the answers to the sub-questions in the conclusion. In this way, taken together, the answers to the sub-questions answer the main question.

Sources

Jong, J. de (2011). *Handboek academisch schrijven: In stappen naar een essay, paper of scriptie*. Bussum: Uitgeverij Coutinho.

Oost, H. & Markenhof, A. (2003). *Een onderzoek voorbereiden*. Baarn: HB uitgevers.

6 A testable concept

By formulating relevant indicators and variables, you can make the abstract (concepts and, to a lesser extent, dimensions) concrete. In this chapter, we explain how to do this.

Why operationalize?

It's often the case that abstract concepts and processes are not 'visible'; they only exist on paper as words, not in the form of something that can be described and explained in concrete terms. You therefore need to make these concepts and indicators measurable. In other words, you need to **operationalize** them.

We use the term 'operationalization' to describe the process of transforming abstract ideas in a research field into specific measurable units. This is because concepts such as 'water consumption' and 'problematic drug use' are not visible in themselves and thus cannot be measured directly. All kinds of associations can be made with them. In the case of water consumption, for example, you could think of a household tap, but also of a river. In the case of addiction, you might immediately think of criminality, but perhaps also of overdoses. As there are so many different potential associations, it is impossible to measure this concept directly.

In short, the researcher has to be very precise. How often someone uses drugs, for example, is a first step in defining problematic drug use; but this needs to be specified even further. What do we mean by 'often'? And when do we start referring to 'drug use'? This is the step you make in the final stage of operationalization, when you reflect on the indicators and variables.

Operationalization is also extremely important in the context of interdisciplinary research, because many concepts are multidimensional. By this we mean that they cannot be measured using a single indicator, number, or concept. Operationalization is not only about the *visibility* of a concept, but also about conveying its *complexity*. A good example of this is discussed in *Chapter 4*. Defining 'water use' is multidimensional, certainly if you want to approach the topic from both a natural scientific and a humanities perspective. You therefore need to think carefully about how to make your concepts measurable in a way that includes multiple theoretical perspectives.

From dimensions to indicators and variables

Just like constructing a theoretical framework, operationalization can be done in many different ways. You can get an overview of all the different possibilities by making an **operationalization scheme**. *Box 6.1* shows an example of such a scheme, drawn up for two of the concepts from the literature review in *Appendix A*.

In the sample literature review, you can see clearly how the indicators and variables relate to one another. One dimension of water use is the water that is used to produce a product. The other dimension of water use is the water that is used in the entire production chain. Together, these dimensions make up the water footprint (the core concept). But you're not there yet; for how do you measure the water used for production and in the whole production chain? For convenience's sake, here we have only developed the example of water used for production. This can be measured by looking at the water that ends up in the product itself, at how much water evaporates during the production process, and at the quantity of water that is eventually polluted. After that, however, you still need to establish the value that your indicator will take. In this case, this is the number of cubic metres of water that is needed to produce a ton of a certain product.

Indicators can thus indicate how something should be measured; they are a roadmap, as it were, that you follow from the abstract to the specific. The **variable** is the value that this indicator can eventually assume. In the literature report (*Appendix A*), for example, 'water footprint' (the concept) can be divided into the direct water footprint (dimension), which can be measured, among other things, in terms of the volume of water that ends up in the products themselves (indicator) per m^3/ton of water that is stored in the product (variable) (see *Box 6.1*).

The concepts discussed in *Chapter 4* have been operationalized in *Box 6.1*. In order to show that different disciplines can take rather different approaches, we have added an extra operationalization that contrasts with the examples from the literature review in *Appendix A*. This is because water use can be approached in different ways in the social sciences; there are researchers who see certain forms of water consumption as a form of 'water grabbing', meaning that access to water and the way such access is obtained are extremely important (Franco et al., 2013).

In the context of this research, it would be interesting to examine the extent to which the use of water for meat production undermines access to water elsewhere in the world. This would result in a slightly different indicator; not a volume that can be expressed numerically, but social rules and legal norms that are expressed more qualitatively. The 'variable' field has thus been left blank in this operationalization, not because it is impossible to transform these indicators into variables, but because it is probably better to measure such indicators qualitatively (more on this in *Chapter 7*).

Box 6.1   *From dimensions to indicators*

Theory	Concept	Dimensions	Indicator	Variable
Meat production, soya production, and water use	Water footprint (Ercin et al., 2012) = total volume of fresh water that is used directly or indirectly to produce a product	Direct water footprint (water consumed in the production of a certain product)	Volume of water that ends up in the products themselves	m³/ton of water stored in product X
			Volume of water that evaporates during the production process	m³/ton of water that evaporates during the production of product X
			Volume of water that is polluted by waste water left by factory	m³/ton of water that is polluted as a result of the production of product X
		Indirect water footprint (water consumption in whole production chain)		
	'Water grabbing' (Franco et al., 2013)	Access to water	Informal property rights	
			Formal property rights	

Operationalization and validity

In order to achieve an optimal operationalization, it is insufficient simply to draw up a scheme like the one above. As you do your research, it is important to keep casting a critical eye over the choices you've made. Ask yourself questions about the **validity** of your indicator; that is to say, does it measure what you want to measure? After all, it's quite a step to go from abstract concepts to measurable units. Sometimes you'll make an erroneous association, or you'll formulate an indicator in such a way that it no longer measures your concept as precisely as you'd defined it. In the case of water use, for example, things could go horribly wrong if you were to refer only to 'consumption' in your indicators, and forget to include other possible forms of use.

As a result, you not only need to set out your operationalization scheme from left to right, but you should also go over your steps again from right to left, to check that everything you've done still makes sense. Reflect carefully on the choices you've made, and think about whether they are justified. And when you write up your research (see *Part 3*), try to substantiate these choices well. When choosing dimensions and indicators and writing them down, it is essential to look at how this has been done in other research – and link your own research to this (even if only partially). There is no need to reinvent the wheel, and by citing other research, you anchor your operationalization in the literature. In this way, you avoid a certain degree of bias and tunnel vision.

Other forms of operationalization

The process of operationalization that we've described above is a useful way to structure your research and steer it from the abstract to the measurable. It is not the only way to do this, though. There are clear differences in how qualitative and quantitative research studies are operationalized (see *Chapter 8*). In the social sciences, there are also researchers who start with data and base their theory on this, rather than starting with theory and working towards a measurable unit. This is known as *grounded theory*.

There are also various research schools in the humanities and social sciences that operationalize in a slightly less rigid way; they use concepts to do research, but do not go so far as to make them into indicators and variables. In literary and cultural studies, there is often an exchange between theories and concepts and a certain subject of research (a book or a film, for example). Theories on trauma processing, for example, may be discussed in relation to a particular book or film. Concepts are thereby used implicitly to make these theories 'visible' in the subjects of the research, but not as explicitly as in an operationalization scheme. For researchers and students from these disciplines, however, practising with operationalization schemes can also be a helpful 'finger exercise'. Moreover, it can form a useful prelude to interdisciplinary cooperation (see also the introduction to this chapter).

Many disciplines go through the operationalization process only implicitly or partially. In the natural sciences (among others), some researchers work with existing indices and methods, meaning that they do not need to go through all of the steps themselves. However, this is not to say that it is not useful for a natural scientist to reflect on his or her research design in this way. Reflecting on how the index that you are using has been constructed helps you to map out the assumptions and limits of your own research more effectively, and find out where other perspectives could connect or contribute.

Sources

Franco, J., Mehta, L., en Veldwisch, G.J. (2013). The Global Politics of Water Grabbing. *Third World Quarterly, 34*(9), 1651-75.

7 Making a research instrument

After you have operationalized your concepts, it is time to think about your **research instrument**; in other words, how can you determine which instrument you're going to use to measure your indicator or indicators? There are a great many kinds of research instruments to choose from: from lab research to ethnographic fieldwork, and from document analysis to soil research. In the humanities, social sciences, and natural sciences, different approaches require different research instruments.

Quantitative instruments require a technical specification that can be different for each research specialization, and for this, we refer you to the specialist literature that you'll use in your course's methodology modules. Although this is also true of qualitative instruments, there is a common basis for making instruments for this type of research, meaning that this is easier to explain. That's not to say, though, that quantitative research isn't covered at all in this book; the sample research article at the back of the book (see *Appendix B*) is based on quantitative research, and in Part 3 we look at the correct way to display quantitative data.

Qualitative versus quantitative

What is **qualitative research** and what is **quantitative research**? There are many misunderstandings about this. It is sometimes claimed, for example, that quantitative research is objective and qualitative research is subjective. This distinction doesn't hold, however: although qualitative research investigates data that are often subjective in nature, this does not detract from the objectivity of the research itself.

What's more, quantitative research has always suffered from the stigma that it is 'more difficult' than qualitative research. Quantitative research does admittedly require a large set of skills, and statistics tends to inspire fear in many students. Compared to this, doing interviews, a feature of much qualitative research, might seem a breeze. But nothing could be further from the truth. Organizing, conducting, transcribing, and analysing interviews is by no means less complicated than, say, gathering, preparing, and analysing large statistical datasets. One factor here is that you're often unable to fall back on standardized methods and software, but instead have to figure a lot out for yourself.

What is the difference, then? In qualitative research, the emphasis lies on understanding what is specific to a research group or a research subject. Qualitative research often makes use of observations and in-depth interviews. This means that you probe in as much depth as you can during the data collection, so that you can produce as precise a picture of the respondent as possible. These data are subsequently ordered by coding; that is, by searching for patterns between the respondents. By observing and talking at length with a small group of respondents, you build up a detailed picture of all of the aspects that are important – but only for this (often small) group. Based on these data, the researcher then looks at what general lessons can be drawn, but often the objective is not to generalize the qualitative research; rather, it is to get a better understanding of the specific dynamic of the research problem.

By contrast, quantitative research allows you to make generalizations; statements about whole populations that are generally valid. For qualitative research, this is more difficult. In quantitative research, numerical data (or other kinds of data that have been converted into figures) are gathered and analysed. Based on this numerical knowledge, you can make statements, for example about possible patterns, averages, or relationships. In order to do this, you need a research group with more respondents, because many statistical measures are only meaningful when they apply to a larger population. In this case, then, you are primarily interested in the *general*, or what all of the respondents or subjects of the research have in common.

The decision to carry out qualitative or quantitative research should thus be based on what you want to get out of your subjects of inquiry. You start with a different kind of data source. In the case of quantitative research, you assume that the data can be found in what a whole population or a whole series of research subjects have in common. In the case of qualitative research, you assume that the data are contained in your research subjects themselves. The knowledge is located in particular individuals, and they are able to share it. In short, whether you go for a quantitative or a qualitative research design is purely a methodological choice that is dictated by precisely *what* you want to know and *why*.

When qualitative and when quantitative?

For most research in the natural sciences, it is pretty clear that the only option available is a quantitative option – either because the data and the methods that you are building on are quantitative, or because the generalization of data is extremely important in the natural sciences. On the other hand, this does not automatically mean that research in the humanities and social sciences is always qualitative. Linguists, for example, often use quantitative questionnaires, and an increasing amount of quantitative research is also being done in the social sciences (for example, in psychology and sociology). In these disciplines, certainly when they intersect in interdisciplinary research – where the humanities, social sciences, and natural sciences come together – it is difficult to see when you should choose a qualitative design and when you should choose a quantitative one. In this section,

Box 7.1   An operationalization diagram for the concepts of 'cognitive control' and 'problematic drug use' used in the sample research article in Appendix B

Concept	Dimension	Indicator	Question/Item	Outcome measure (variable/score/topic, etc.)
Cognitive control	Attentional processes	Degree of attentional bias for incorrect colour and word combination (for example, green printed in yellow ink)		Speed in the case of incorrect colour/word combination (slower means less cognitive control)
	Memory processes			
Problematic drug use	Characteristics of dependence on a substance*	Number of failed attempts to reduce or control cannabis use	Questionnaire (part of CUDIT) Over the last six months, how often did you notice that you were unable to stop using cannabis after starting to use it?	Score from 0-4: • Never • Less than monthly • Monthly • Weekly • Daily or almost daily
	The use itself	Frequency of drug use	Questionnaire (part of CUDIT) How often do you use cannabis?	Score from 0-4: • Never • Monthly or less • 2-4 times a month • 2-3 times a week • 4 or more times a week

* This is only one possible characteristic of addiction (abuse or dependence). For reasons of comprehensibility, it was decided not to include all the characteristics here.

we give you a number of tips for making this choice, based on your sample, your choice of research design, and the operationalization of your concepts.

Operationalization

You often choose the type of research instrument you need – qualitative or quantitative – when you operationalize your concepts. Take the example of the research article: in this, the researchers utilize an *experimental design* that uses different types of quantitative research measures, namely an experiment and an interview with questionnaires (surveys). The question is: why is the interview quantitative here, and not qualitative?

If we look at the operationalization of problematic drug use (*Box 7.1*), it becomes clear why the authors opted for quantitative research. Two dimensions of drug use are distinguished: the use itself, and the different characteristics of dependence on a substance. One indicator that can show the latter, for example, is the number of fruitless attempts that an individual has made to stop using drugs. If you measure this, you are measuring whether someone is showing a characteristic of addiction, and you have thereby measured a dimension of problematic drug use. The obvious question is: should we then use a qualitative or quantitative instrument to measure this? In which case, you must first ask: where are the valuable data here? Are we concerned with the individual experience of the drug user, the precise dynamic of one drug user's addiction? Or is this about a whole series of experiences taken together?

In this study, you want to discover the relationship between problematic drug use and cognitive control. The main implication of this is that you want to measure both a respondent's problematic drug use and their cognitive control; and, above all, you want to be able to make generalizable statements about this that apply to a whole population group. Thus, the research is not really about one individual's specific experiences, simply because these are rarely generalizable. If you had wanted to do research into one specific type of drug user's experience of their attempts to quit in a specific context, then qualitative research would have been an option here.

Nowadays, it is increasingly common for researchers to combine qualitative and quantitative research. In such cases, we refer to **mixed methods**. In *interdisciplinary research*, this is certainly a very significant addition to the research palette, because it allows us to link more qualitative and more quantitative-oriented disciplines. Thus, you could have an anthropologist do supplementary qualitative research into a specific population of drug users in order to reveal other possible causal mechanisms. Specific aspects are then combined with the possibility of generalization.

Structure of the instrument

One key factor that plays a role in the choice of qualitative or quantitative research is whether you want to use a standardized instrument that takes a rigorous approach to the data, or want to use a design with more freedom. This is known as the distinction between a **structured** and a **semi-structured** instrument. Fully structured instruments are only really used in quantitative research. In this case, you use fixed questions, a fixed order, and a fixed set of possible answers. Doing structured interviews in qualitative research often means using a questionnaire that is completely fixed, both in terms of content and order, but the answer options are completely open. By contrast, a 'semi-structured' interview is even 'looser'. Here, neither the questions nor the order is completely fixed. Researchers often work with loosely formulated **topic lists** (see section containing *Box 7.2*), which they can use differently depending on how the interview is going.

The degree of structure in your research instrument is entirely dependent on what you want to research and your expectations of the respondents. Again, a key factor is whether you want to make a statement about a population, or whether you want to find out something specific about one or more respondents within a population.

Determining your sample

Another important consideration to make when choosing a quantitative or qualitative instrument is determining your respondents, also known as **sampling**. Don't underestimate this part! Aside from the fact that it is sometimes hard to find respondents (either because it is hard to find respondents who can 'measure' your concept or because it is hard to contact them), it is also important to make a reasoned decision about the **sample** you want to use.

By sample, we mean the individuals you select from a population in order to interview them. This is particularly important for studies in which you try to generalize your results broadly, something that plays a particular role in quantitative research. In that case, your sample needs to be representative of the population you want to say something about. In qualitative research, too, it is important to have a good sample, because you need be able to substantiate why the respondents you have chosen are suitable for answering your research question and measuring the concepts you have operationalized.

In quantitative research, use is often (but not always) made of **random sampling**. That is to say, you attempt to make a random selection from a large population. For example, you could identify a list of a thousand potential respondents and randomly select a number of them using a computer program. This helps you to avoid a degree of **selection bias**, whereby you nevertheless choose certain respondents, consciously or unconsciously.

By contrast, in qualitative research, **non-random sampling** is often (but not always) used. That is because in qualitative research you are often searching for targeted research subjects, not because they reflect a broader population, but because they are relevant subjects to be interviewed. There is a risk of bias here too, though, meaning that it is always important to explain clearly how you selected the respondents.

Random sampling is sometimes confused with non-random sampling methods. Take the example of **convenience sampling**; in this case, you choose your respondents based on the degree of access you have to them. After all, if you are doing research on the European Commission as part of an internship and you already have a network there, it makes sense to use it. And if you subsequently need more respondents and you ask the people in your network whether they happen to know other relevant individuals, this is known as **snowball sampling**. Both are legitimate, so long as you explain your method clearly and show why it is appropriate for your research purposes, and you also reflect on the limits of this sampling in the discussion section (see *Chapter 9*). Although there might seem to be a certain randomness to these two methods, this randomness is not absolute; the researcher has nevertheless made a conscious selection, meaning that these are not cases of random sampling.

Making a qualitative research instrument

Many forms of qualitative research are possible. In the humanities, we come across all kinds of forms of document analysis and analysis of objects, cultural or otherwise. In the social sciences, qualitative research can vary from ethnographic research to expert interviews, focus groups, and design research (where you no longer merely describe and explain reality, but also try to change it).

In this book, we discuss a qualitative method for conducting and analysing interviews on an empirical, structured basis, because this gives a useful indication of the structured, systematic approach that is required by all research, including qualitative research. Once again, this is done using an operationalization scheme (*Box 7.2*). Running through this process is a good exercise in qualitative scholarship, even if you end up focusing more on other kinds of research, because conducting interviews is a systematic form of interaction in which you generate data relating to one or more people. In short, by going through this method, you lay a good foundation that will come in handy as a scientist or scholar.

Formulating interview questions

From indicators to topic lists or questionnaires

When formulating a research instrument, you start from your operationalization scheme; in this case, we go back to the scheme that we set out in in *Box 7.1*. Suppose that you want to approach your research qualitatively. Then you can do one of two things: either you can draw up a **topic list**, a list of potential topics to be discussed, or you can draw up a list of possible questions. It is also possible to combine the two. *Box 7.2* shows a topic list for the operationalization scheme mentioned above, combined with a list of possible questions. It is essential to ensure that the topics in your topic list or the questions in your questionnaire are directly related to one or more indicators of the dimensions that you want to measure.

Box 7.2   Example of a topic list for the operationalization scheme in Box 7.1

Topic list	Possible questions
Duration of use	How long have you been using cannabis? How old were you when you first tried cannabis? When did you start using it on a weekly/daily basis?
Addiction characteristic: limited control over use	Have you ever tried to stop using cannabis? Did you succeed? How long did you refrain from using it? How often have you tried to stop? Do you think about cannabis when you are not under the influence? Do you feel like using it?
Addiction characteristic: interpersonal problems related to use	Do the people around you say anything about your use? Have you ever stayed home from work/college because you were under the influence?

Order of the questionnaire

When you interview someone, you obviously want the respondent to be optimally placed to answer the questions. This means that the phrasing of the questions is important, of course, but also the order in which you ask them, also known as the **route** In general, you should always start by asking questions that are relatively easy to answer; questions that make few demands of one's cognitive abilities, and that cause as little embarrassment as possible. In this way, you avoid situations in which people switch off early in an interview, either because they find the questions too difficult or because they feel uneasy. You can then gradually introduce more difficult questions. Remember that it is also smart to **cluster questions thematically**. In other words, it is best to group together questions that measure a single concept. This will allow your respondents to go more deeply into a topic.

Aside from the structure, the questions themselves are also important. First of all, you need to formulate your questions carefully. Your questions may reflect all kinds of unspoken preferences, and they can quickly become too directive. *Box 7.3* sets out a number of things to watch out for when formulating your questions.

Box 7.3   *Tips for interview questions (adapted from Assen & Van der Ark, n.d.)*

Use simple words	Don't include any terms in your questions that require particular prior knowledge. Avoid using jargon and academic language, which may scare off your respondent. Moreover, your respondent may not fully understand such terms.
Be specific and avoid vague terms	Try to avoid using vague terms, such as 'often', 'regularly' or 'sometimes'. Be aware that 'vague' is not the same as 'open'. By 'vague', we mean terms that appear to indicate specificity when they do not in fact do so. It is fine to ask an open question, whereby your respondent is free to give an associative answer. It is confusing, though, to ask your respondents a seemingly specific question when the terms you use can be interpreted in different ways. After all, what is 'often'? Once a week? Once a month? Once in a lifetime? If you want to know something in particular, such as a date, time or location, be as specific as possible in how you ask the question.
Avoid long, complicated sentences	Try to avoid using negative terms whenever possible (*not, nothing, nobody, no, never*), and never use double negations ('not unjustifiably', 'no negative feelings', etc.). In addition, try to maximize your use of short sentences. Questions that consist of main and subordinate clauses can best be split into separate questions. Always remember that the more clearly a question is asked, the closer the answer will be to the researcher's intentions – and that is ultimately what it is all about.

Once your questionnaire is complete and you've made sure that your questions are valid and reliable (see next section) and follow a good 'route', it is time to think about the interviews themselves. For this, it is useful to make an **interview script**. A script is a kind of action plan for your interview, including the planning, topic list, background information on the respondents, the logistics of the interview, and so forth. This helps to ensure the interview goes well, but it is also a useful resource for when you eventually write up your methods section. Be sure to take this script with you to the interview; if something goes wrong, you'll have all the key information to hand.

Validity and reliability of your instrument

Regardless of whether you're doing qualitative or quantitative research, your research instrument needs to be reliable and valid.

When you have finished your instrument (or if you've opted for an existing instrument), you should look closely at the instrument's **reliability**. That is to say: could your instrument be used such that the research could be carried out twice in an identical way? This is comparable to a weighing scale. A small deviation is permissible, but the scale is not reliable if you suddenly find yourself 5 kilograms heavier in one day. This is important, because the replicability of research will otherwise be brought into question. When doing scholarly research, another researcher should always be able to **replicate** your research; that is, follow your steps precisely to see whether the same result is achieved. It is essential to have a good and reliable instrument for this.

In addition, it is important to consider the **validity** of your instrument. Validity concerns the meaning of the outcome: does the instrument indeed measure what you want to know? It can be divided into internal and external validity; the **internal validity** is high if your instrument directly measures the outcome measure without there being possible third variables that could cause background noise or explain the relationship. In other words, does the instrument measure what you want it to measure? One example is that of the Eleven-plus exam to determine a primary school pupil's secondary-school level (in England and Northern Ireland). Does this effectively measure a pupil's skills in spelling, arithmetic, and so forth?

In addition, there is **external validity**; that is to say, the degree of generalizability. This is particularly important in quantitative research (but qualitative research also tries to make generalizing statements at times). In other words: can the data you gathered during the experiment be generalized to everyday practice? Is a stress test in a lab comparable with work or study stress, and can conclusions thus be drawn from this? And if you have a sample that contains only psychology students, can you draw conclusions from this about the entire population of a country?

When it comes to external validity, it is important to check carefully that you have a good sample; that is, that you have chosen the right respondents and that no bias has crept in. If you are conducting an interview, you need to look carefully at the formulation of your questions. Are they overly directive? If so, this can lead to **reactivity**. In this case, the respondents may behave in a socially desirable way and say what they think you, the researcher, want to hear. This can undermine the generalizability of your results.

For both reliability and internal validity, it is important to keep a close eye on your operationalization scheme to make sure that your question really is measuring the concept that you want to measure. One good exercise here is to think up the answers that might be given to your question. Do these answers come close to the concept that you want to measure? Or have you actually drifted away from where you started? You should also try to keep a proper record of the steps you took when operationalizing and making the questionnaire.

Assessment by an ethics committee

It is standard for experiments involving human and animal subjects to be submitted to the department or university's ethics committee for approval *before* the research takes place. Student research carried out within a discipline also falls under the responsibility of the ethics committee, which is why you should always submit your research design to your lecturer before making a start on the empirical research.

The exact form that a request to an ethics committee should take is different for each faculty and type of research (take a careful look at the ethical requirements of the faculty where you are doing your research). In general, the application should clearly state exactly what you want to research. In the case of research involving human test subjects, you need to submit an **information brochure** that the test subject can read before the research. Test subjects should to be able to make out from this brochure what the research will involve in terms of burden, risk or discomfort, whether there is some form of reward, that their contribution is voluntary, and that their anonymity is guaranteed.

This information should be accompanied by an **informed consent** that is signed by the test subject, should they wish to take part in the research having read the brochure. If you are giving test subjects misleading information about the research (as is done in some psychological experiments), there are additional provisions, such as a full debriefing to explain how test subjects were misled, and the possible negative consequences of this deception should be taken into consideration.

In the methods section of the sample article in *Appendix B*, you can see how this ethical component can be recorded in your article: 'The study was approved by the ethics committee of the Academic Medical Centre (AMC) in Amsterdam and informed consent forms were signed by all participants'.

Sources

Assen, M.A.L.M., & Van der Ark, L.A. (n.d.). Vuistregels voor het formuleren van vragen. Geraadpleegd op https://www.tilburguniversity.edu/upload/ f25c6b16-d0e5-4c97-bfe6-78ac661a7fe8

Cronbach, L.J., & Meehl, P.E. (1955). Construct validity in psychological tests. *Psychological Bulletin, 52*(4), 281-302.

Other useful sources

A good overview of types of validity can be found in:

- Graziano, A.M., & Raulin, M.L. (2010). *Research methods: a process of inquiry (5th edition)*. Boston: Pearson Education Inc., publishing as Allyn & Bacon.

8 Research practice

After doing your literature review, you decided upon your research question. Next, you operationalized the concepts from your question, and came up with a research method and instruments to study this question. Now it's time for the next step: research practice. Whether you are doing qualitative or quantitative research, there are ways to ensure that you gather data in a scholarly manner.

Research practice: quantitative research

Safeguarding the validity of quantitative research

Before you start doing your research, when doing quantitative research, there are a number of things that you should bear in mind to maximize the validity. Of course, you can ensure that you select good, valid instruments that measure what you want to measure (see *Chapter 7*), but you can also take a number of additional measures that relate to the design of your research. The information below (see also *Box 8.1*) is based on Graziano and Raulin (2010) and applies to research with an experimental design (as opposed to research with a non-experimental design).

With an **experimental design**, you: 1) compare an experimental group with a control group; 2) manipulate a variable (see *Chapter 6*) within this experimental group; and/ or 3) randomly assign test subjects to the experimental or control group. By contrast, research with a **non-experimental design** does not meet one or more of these conditions. An example of this is a case study, in which a person or a group of people is followed for a certain amount of time. See the research article in *Appendix B* for a good example of an experimental design, in which a group of test subjects who use drugs is compared to a group of test subjects who do not. In this case, the second group is the **control group**. By '**manipulating**' a variable, we mean that you compare the groups and then change the conditions for one of the groups. For example, you give a medicine to one group of participants and see what happens.

If you use an experimental design in which you manipulate a variable and see what happens, it is important for the groups to be as similar as possible before the manipulation. In other words: all of the disruptive factors should be equal between the groups. Suppose, for example, that your research question is about the effect of stress on memory. You want to test this by giving a group of people a stress test, but not giving the control group the test. Suppose that the control group were to consist of people with a stressful job and the individuals in the experimental group were all on holiday; you can imagine that this would give rise to problems when interpreting your results. This can be avoided by **randomizing** your test subjects; in other words, assigning them to one of the two groups by drawing lots. The idea behind this is that the disruptive factors will then be similar for the two groups (assuming that your groups are large enough), meaning that any difference between the groups can be attributed to your manipulation.

If you use an experimental design without manipulation, as is done in the research article in *Appendix B*, randomization is not possible, of course. In this case, the variable that you are interested in (drug use) is not manipulated, but formed the criterion for inclusion in the experimental group that test subjects had to meet. In such cases, it is important to **match** the control group to your experimental group. For example, you can ensure that there are equal numbers of men and women in both groups, and that both groups have the same level of education. Again, this ensures that these factors will no longer have any influence on the relationship that you want to investigate.

Finally, you can ensure that your participants and/or the test leader do not know which groups the participants are in. This is called making your participants and/ or your test leader 'blind'. A distinction is made between **single blind** (only the participants are blind) and **double blind** (both the participants and the test leader are blind). In this way, you prevent the expectations of the participant or the test leader from influencing your outcome measure. A good example of this is the placebo effect: if people expect a medicine or medical treatment to work, they are also more likely to experience this. The placebo effect can be obviated by preventing participants from working out which condition they are in.

Box 8.1 *An overview of the measures that can be taken in relation to the design of your research, based on Graziano and Raulin (2010)*

Experimental design		You make choices in relation to:
Experimental group vs. control group	With manipulation	Randomization/blinding
	Without manipulation	Matching
Cross-sectional design	Measuring the groups in one time period	Any differences between the groups could be the result of various factors, so you need to identify these and figure out how you are going to monitor them
Longitudinal (pre-test post-test) design	Measuring the groups at multiple points in time	This is more work, but there is a greater chance that the group difference is a result of your manipulation

Keeping a log

In both qualitative and quantitative research, data are often collected over a long period of time, and data are also frequently gathered by several people. This means that it's crucial to keep a good record of every step and decision. This is commonly done in a **log** (or lab journal, as it is known in the biomedical sciences). Try to get used to keeping a record of the steps in your thinking as you analyse your results. For example, it may be extremely logical to delete a test subject's data from the database on the grounds that the measurement failed, but two months later, you may no longer know precisely what you did and why. Noting down these kinds of decisions is essential for eventually being able to write up your research in a clear and replicable way.

With (historical) **source research** in the humanities, for example, it is important to account for any numbers, facts, or anecdotes that you analyse as 'data'. It can thus be handy to keep a log during the research that includes the source you found, the author, the page, in what department of which archive, and how you found it. After all, it is important for the validity of your research that another researcher is able to retrace your steps. You should also be aware of the **hermeneutic** and the **double hermeneutic**. The 'hermeneutic' refers to the fact that the data that are taken from a source are themselves an interpretation of a certain (social) phenomenon. The 'double hermeneutic' means that if you take these data and put them in a new context, you are also creating your own new interpretation of the facts. Making a note of the context of the source, where you found it, when, and so forth, will allow you to defend your interpretations later, when accounting for the sources you have used. You could also use the literature matrix for this, for example (or a variant of it; see *Chapter 2*).

Organizing your data

As well as organizing your data, you need to think about its **ethical aspects**, especially if you have gathered sensitive information or are working with vulnerable test subjects such as children or patients. Ensure that your data are stored in a secure environment, or secure your files with a password (this is possible for folders, for example, or separate Microsoft files). In addition, **anonymize** the data by deleting the personal details from your files and attributing test subject numbers.

It is also important to **clean up your data**. Sometimes minor errors are made when entering data (capital letters, punctuation, typos), meaning that the data are not presented in the way that was originally intended. Most software that is used to process and analyse data (Excel, for example) includes good search tools for catching errors. Don't forget to save the original data file, however, just in case something goes wrong when you're cleaning it up.

Getting familiar with your data

As soon as you have completed your data collection, you will have a file of figures that you will need to interpret. All being well, you can use these data to answer your research question, and you will have already reflected on the statistics you need to interpret them (which you did when formulating your hypothesis). Before you do this, however, it is important to represent your data graphically (to **plot** them). Make as many plots in as many ways as you can, in order to reveal patterns and recognize outliers.

Once you understand how your data fit together, you can go on to the next step: statistical testing in order to answer your research question. It goes without saying that you should not adjust your research question to fit your findings (**data fishing**) or leave out data points that do not fit in your hypothesized pattern. The latter is a form of **data massaging**, whereby you adjust your data until you get the desired results. Both data fishing and data massaging are types of fraud (see *Chapter 12*).

In statistics, a rough dichotomy can be made between classical (frequentist) statistics and Bayesian statistics. At present, the most widely used statistics are classical statistics. These have a number of disadvantages, however, prompting increasing calls for more use of Bayesian statistics. It lies beyond the scope of this book to go into this, but if you need to decide which form of statistics or specific test to use, it is important to consider this in depth (see '*Other useful sources*' at the end of this chapter for helpful literature).

Social scientific research can take many forms: ethnographic, focus groups, participatory observation, and many more. But all of these methods have one thing in common: structured interaction with the subjects of inquiry. Setting up and conducting interviews is a skill that is important for all of these methods, which is why we develop the example from *Chapter 7* in this chapter to illustrate how to do qualitative research.

Before the interview

In *Chapter 7*, we already explained in detail how to make a research instrument. Such an instrument can do many things, but it doesn't provide ready-made respondents. Exactly how you find your respondents largely depends on the context of your research and the respondents you need (see 'sampling' in *Chapter 7*). In addition, it is mainly about taking the initiative, keeping asking questions, and persevering if things don't work out immediately.

On the whole, people consider it an honour to be interviewed. People like talking about something that's close to their heart or that they know a lot about, whether it's in their personal life or part of their job. You can appeal to this by emphasizing the unique knowledge they have or the special insight they could offer you into your topic. Always be clear about the purpose of your research and the form it will take (any publications).

Once you have found someone who is prepared to give an interview, it is important to make agreements beforehand about a whole range of ethical and practical issues, to avoid any misunderstandings. Ensure that you record these agreements/considerations in your log straight away, so you have everything in black and white. In *Box 8.2*, you will find a checklist that you can use to prepare for your interview.

During the interview

Interviews are rather paradoxical activities. On the one hand, you want to allow the respondent to say as much as possible in as much detail as possible. You often achieve this by asking open and descriptive questions based on your topic list, and by giving the respondent lots of space to dwell on them. On the other hand, of course, you want what you are told by the respondent to be comprehensible to the researcher. This means that you should occasionally reflect on what the respondent says, and pay slightly more attention to his phrasing. That is when you start **probing**; in other words, you keep asking questions.

According to Taylor et al. (2016), keeping asking questions is the difference between interviewing and 'normal' conversations. In most conversations, you fill in much of the meaning of the other person's words yourself. If a fellow student says that he thinks a subject is stupid, you have a rough idea of what he means by 'stupid'. As an interviewer, you sometimes think you know these sorts of things, but it is important to keep questioning nevertheless, because you may think certain things are obvious when this is not actually the case.

Box 8.2   Key points for preparing for interviews (source: Taylor et al., 2016)

Anonymity	Make clear agreements about whether you are allowed to include someone's name in your work, or whether you should use a pseudonym. If someone is happy to be named, but you suspect that this may cause problems for them or may even be dangerous, it is your duty as a researcher to point this out.
Recording	In order to be able to process the interview data effectively, you often need an audio recording of the conversation. You should inform the respondent of this in advance, and they naturally have the right to refuse – so always bring a pen and paper with you.
The final say	Some interviewees want to review the interview report before it is published and reserve the right to make changes. This can mean that you no longer measure what you want to measure: it can undermine the validity of your research. You should thus ensure that you make clear agreements beforehand about how and whether you will incorporate the respondent's comments.
Payment	Sometimes it is necessary to provide a certain honorarium in exchange for an interview (money or study credits). This is not ideal, as having external motivation may cause the respondents to give the answers they think you want to hear. In some cases, however, this is the only way to get to speak to someone.
Location	The interview obviously needs to be conducted somewhere. This could be your own office or the university, but it could also be someone's home, the street, or even a public place such as a cafe or restaurant. In any case, ensure that there is nothing in the surroundings that could influence or distract the respondent, that it is quiet enough to record the conversation in sufficient quality, and that the respondent is able to speak freely.

In short, as an interviewer, you regularly need to ask the respondent to clarify information in order to go into it in more depth. It can be a good idea to rephrase what the respondent has just said in your own words, and then ask whether they could confirm this: 'So, by stupid, you mean not challenging enough?' But you shouldn't take this rephrasing too far. Ideally, you want a situation in which the respondent is speaking most of the time and you steer them as little as possible. Thus try, as a researcher, to keep an eye on what you say at all times. Moreover, you should always be sensitive and never judgemental.

After the interview

The relationship between interview data and 'the truth' is not entirely straightforward. On the one hand, by using established procedures, questionnaires and/or topics, based on concepts and indicators, you try to guarantee the reliability and the validity of your research. On the other hand, your respondents bring a certain degree of subjectivity, and that is fine. After all, you want to sketch out the experiences and thoughts of your respondents in as much detail as possible, so long as you ensure that they are somewhat consistent in their answers. For this reason, too, it is important to keep probing during the interview in order to focus and clarify the answers as much as possible, and to study your data carefully afterwards.

In addition to this check, it is important to record your interview in text form, which you do by **transcribing** it. When you have made recordings, this can often be done using a computer. There are various software programs for this; some have to be purchased, others are free (for example, Google Docs has a free system). What this software should be able to do, in any case, is play the audio file at a slower speed, so that you have time to write it down at your own pace. Be aware that you should make a note of everything when transcribing; in principle, every cough and every hesitation is data. Ultimately, the resulting text file (the **transcript**, see *Box 8.3* for an example) is the collection of data that you will analyse. You should also bear in mind that transcribing can take rather a long time. Depending on your experience, typing speed, and so forth, a one-hour recording will often take four or five hours to transcribe. So be sure to reserve time for this when planning your research!

Box 8.3   *Example of a transcript*

Interviewer:	'Have you, er, ever previously had to deal with, um, say, drug use in the family?'
Respondent:	'[3 seconds of silence] Yes, um, I don't really know about that. I do have an uncle who, er [coughs several times], did have some trouble of that sort, I believe, yes.

Analysing the interview

The transcript is by no means the end product that you will hand in and present. First, these data need to be analysed, and this can be done by **coding**. This is the process in which you try to link your concepts to your data in order to find meaningful patterns, similarities and contrasts. These could be patterns between your respondents themselves, or between your interview data and the theoretical framework.

Coding is not only done in the social sciences; humanities scholars often analyse and code their data at text level, too (for example, in discourse analysis). But there are also humanities and social sciences scholars who analyse texts or audio-visual material at word level, even though they wouldn't call it this or use this systematic method. That is why we are focusing on coding here, because it is an excellent method for guaranteeing the reliability and validity of research.

How does coding work? Much of the methodological literature distinguishes between three phases. First of all, there is the **open coding** phase. In this phase, you look carefully at your transcript and scrutinize your respondents' answers. The statements can be labelled and these labels form your first codes. Much of the methodological literature (for example, Berg, 2000; Given, 2008) suggests that you streamline this process with a new set of questions; this time, these are used to interrogate the data, not the respondent. See *Box 8.4* for examples of such questions.

It is essential that you let the data speak. Try not to add categories that you have defined in advance, and only make codes that come directly from the data. This is a rough process in which you, the researcher, are free to begin broadly without losing sight of the objective of your research.

Box 8.4   Examples of underlying questions for open coding (Given, 2008)

What is happening?
Which actions have been performed or described?
How were these actions performed?
By whom?
With what underlying purpose?
What was the meaning of this? What was the reason for this?
Which feelings or thoughts are communicated?

After the open coding, you move on to **axial coding**. You thereby cast a critical eye over your initial list of codes and try to work out where the overlaps are, which codes prove irrelevant on closer reflection, and which codes can be reworded and merged. *Box 8.5* contains an example of fictitious data. First, a broad sketch is made of the catchwords that are important for this piece of data; then the similarities and differences between the codes are considered.

Box 8.5 *Fictitious example of an interview and possible open and axial codes*

Text fragment	Open coding	Axial coding
'Drugs made me feel powerful, like I could take on the whole world.'	Power. Able to take on the world.	Self-image, need to perform.
'I started using to numb my feelings, to forget my sadness.'	Numb. Sadness. Forgetting.	Processing.
'My self-esteem at work was very low, but drugs changed that.'	Low self-esteem. Change in self-esteem.	Self-image, need to perform.
'I was under a lot of pressure to perform, failure wasn't an option for me. Using drugs gave me a sense of peace.'	Pressure to perform. Failure no option. Peace.	Need to perform, processing.

Finally, you move on to **selective coding**. With this, you try to link your axial codes to the concepts that you wanted to measure. One way of doing this is to make a **coding tree**. See *Figure 8.1* for an example. Unlike the operationalization scheme, the coding tree doesn't run from left to right, but from right to left. You thus reason from your codes back to the concepts and dimensions you identified during the operationalization. In this way, you 'complete the circle'; you have done everything you can to guarantee the reliability and validity of your research.

Figure 8.1 An example of a coding tree

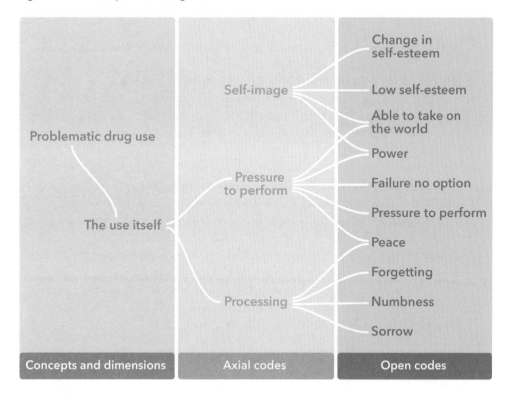

After coding

Your study doesn't end with your coding tree. You can use it now to write the narrative of your analysis; your interpretation of the research data, so to say. Based on the codes that you've found and the relationship between the codes and the theory, you write down your main findings. What patterns can you identify between the respondents? And what contrasts? Do they confirm or negate the theory? In doing so, don't forget to refer clearly to your interview data (see *Chapter 12*).

Sources

Berg, B.L. (2000). *Qualitative research methods for the social sciences (4th edition)*. Boston: Allyn & Bacon.

Given, L.M. (2008). *The Sage encyclopedia of qualitative research methods (2nd edition)*. California: Sage.

Graziano, A.M., & Raulin, M.L. (2010). *Research methods: a process of inquiry (5th edition)*. Boston: Pearson Education Inc., publishing as Allyn & Bacon.

Taylor, S.J., Bogdan, R., & DeVault, M.L. (2016). *Introduction to qualitative research methods. A guidebook and resource (4th edition)*. Hoboken: Wiley.

Other useful sources

To get a broader picture of the ethical issues that arise when gathering and analysing data, you could take a look at the ethical principles of the American Psychological Association (APA):http://www.apa.org/ethics/code/index.aspx.

A good starting point for immersing yourself in the discussion on classical and Bayesian statistics is the podcast by the Human Interaction Laboratory (at Tufts University). Google 'The Bayes factor podcast' and you will find multiple podcasts by academics who use Bayesian statistics (especially Episode 2 with Eric-Jan Wagenmakers is a good introduction into the topic).

When it comes to statistics, there are a great many different options, and the choice of test depends on your research design and data. A lot of literature is available on this, but if you are looking for a good basic book, then the following book by Andy Field is highly recommended:

- Field, A.P. (2017). *Discovering Statistics using IBM SPSS Statistics (5th edition)*. London: Sage Publications LtD.

9 The structure of your article

In this chapter, we first address how to establish a clear argumentation structure. Subsequently, we explain the specific structure of a scholarly text and what is usually included in the introduction, the middle section, and the discussion..

Argumentation structure

A scholarly article can be seen as a line of argument in which you convince the reader of your conclusion, based on your results. As discussed in *Chapter 3*, using an argumentation scheme can help you to break down a text, but it also works the other way around: you can build up your text on the basis of your own argumentation scheme.

The **argumentation structure** is the backbone of your text and the path that you, the writer, mark out for the reader. Thus, it is not the path that you take during your research. Non-fiction books, for example, often advance a viewpoint that is substantiated in the rest of the book in a logical path. But it is unlikely that the author began with this elaborate argumentation structure; they probably drafted it after doing detailed research.

Thus, when writing a text, you shouldn't ask your readers to follow the path that you took; you should spare them the dead-end arguments, the misleading steps, and unnecessary detours. Instead, you should mark out the shortest, most logical route to your question, and subsequently how you got from your results to your conclusion. In interdisciplinary texts in particular, where you need to draw links between different perspectives, it is essential to have a clear argumentation structure.

Establishing a clear structure before you start writing can make it easier to stick to the line of the argument (and you will become less lost in the details). It also becomes easier to see which parts you can delete and where there are still holes in your argument. In *Figure 9.1*, you will find an example of an argument structure like this, based on the literature report in *Appendix A*. In this article, the arguments in favour of the central argument and the arguments that substantiate it are divided into sections (1.1, 1.2, etc.).

Figure 9.1 An example of an argument structure based on the literature review in Appendix A

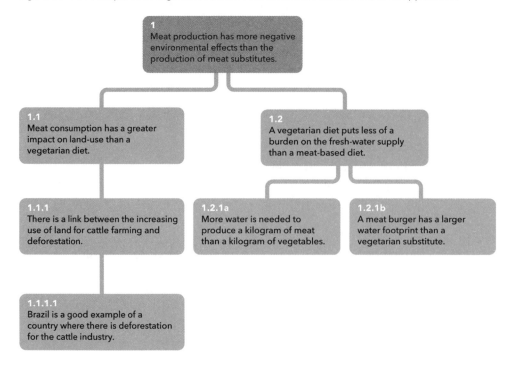

1
Meat production has more negative environmental effects than the production of meat substitutes.

1.1
Meat consumption has a greater impact on land-use than a vegetarian diet.

1.2
A vegetarian diet puts less of a burden on the fresh-water supply than a meat-based diet.

1.1.1
There is a link between the increasing use of land for cattle farming and deforestation.

1.2.1a
More water is needed to produce a kilogram of meat than a kilogram of vegetables.

1.2.1b
A meat burger has a larger water footprint than a vegetarian substitute.

1.1.1.1
Brazil is a good example of a country where there is deforestation for the cattle industry.

Objections

Although you are supposed to indicate the path to the point you wish to make as clearly as possible, this does not mean that you should ignore any evidence that disputes your position. On the contrary, you are expected to reflect on potential objections when drafting a scholarly text. You can use potential objections to make your argument and position more nuanced and stronger, for example in the theoretical framework or the discussion section of a scholarly article. There are two sorts of objections: a denial that the argument itself is correct, or a denial of the link – often implicit – between the argument and the position (see *Chapter 3*).

As the author of a text, it is therefore wise to reflect on potential objections, because **refuting** (or even **negating**) them can strengthen your position. In the article's discussion section, you can refer to both the objection and the refutation. This is done, for example, in the sample text in *Appendix A*. Here, the objection plus the refutation are used to strengthen the author's own position. The author asserts the view that people need to start eating less meat. The whole argument is supported by the findings that in Brazil, more land is needed to cultivate crops for the cattle industry than to produce soya. One counterargument is: 'It is theoretically possible that completely different conclusions could be drawn in other regions and for other products.' The grounds for this objection follow from the argument: 'In the research, we chose to analyse particular regions (Brazil) and particular products (soya burgers).'

The objection can be negated, in turn, by rebutting the counterargument. In the example, the rebuttal is as follows: 'The arguments for eating less meat also apply to other regions and products.' This is because, as follows from the arguments supporting the refutation: 'Cattle will always need feed and a habitat', and: 'A number of kilograms of plant material will always be needed to produce a single kilogram of meat.' See the argumentation structure in *Figure 9.2* for an overview.

Figure 9.2 Example of an argumentation structure based on the literature review in Appendix A, showing both the objections and their refutations

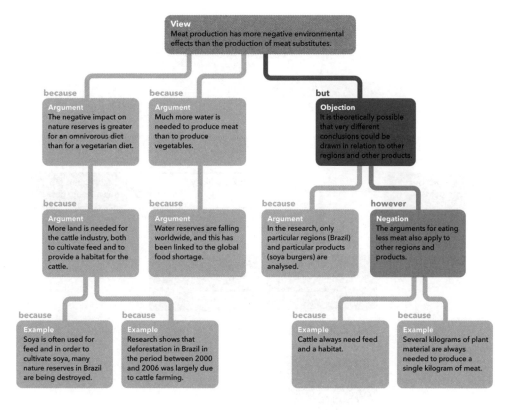

Objections can have an additional impact on your argumentation. In scholarly discussions, objections are often used to add nuance to a viewpoint. The philosopher Stephen Toulmin has developed a model in which an objection is referred to as the 'qualification' (Toulmin, 2003).

Drawing on data, for example, it can be stated that 'Machteld was born in Amsterdam', which leads to the conclusion that she therefore has a Dutch passport. This can be claimed on the grounds that someone who is born in the Netherlands automatically receives a Dutch passport, as provided by the Netherlands Nationality Act. But one can think of exceptions whereby Machteld does not in fact have a Dutch passport; because she has since adopted a different nationality, for example. This is called the qualifier (the 'unless'); it means that you cannot state that Machteld *therefore* has a Dutch passport, but that it is indeed *likely* that she has one. In other words: the objection adds nuance to the argumentation. This is represented in the Toulmin model as follows (*Figure 9.3*):

Figure 9.3 The Toulmin model, an argumentation structure that can be used to add nuance to a position

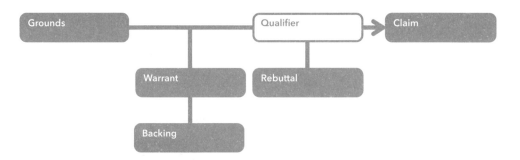

Example of the Toulmin model (based on Stichting Kritisch Denken, 2008)

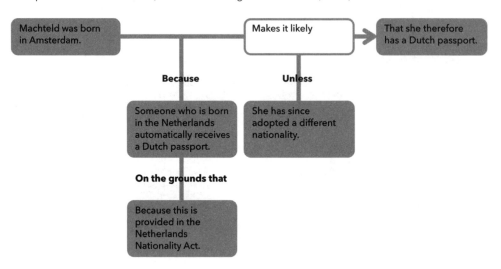

If you read texts this way, you will discover that the links between a position and a conclusion are often implicit. You can imagine someone saying: 'Machteld was born in Amsterdam and therefore she (probably) has a Dutch passport.' The connecting motivation ('someone who is born in the Netherlands gets a Dutch passport') and the backing for this ('as provided in the Netherlands Nationality Act') are sometimes omitted. It can also happen that the basis for the qualifier ('unless she has since adopted another nationality') is not stated explicitly. Although it is important, when drafting an argument, to make the foundations of the argument as explicit as possible, when writing a text, the need for efficiency comes into play and there are some general assumptions that you won't write down explicitly.

Framing an argument: pitfalls

When framing an argument, it is important to make it as clear and solid as possible. In doing so, watch out for the invalid arguments or 'fallacies' that can easily slip into texts. Fallacies may seem plausible at first glance, but they certainly don't improve an argument. Based on the experiences of several lecturers who were involved in the creation of this book, we have selected the most common fallacies (see *Box 9.1*).

Box 9.1   *Examples of various fallacies*

	Description	Example
Circular reasoning	When you repeat your position rather than substantiating it with an argument.	For example, if you say that a plan is bad, 'because it is simply no good'.
Appeal to an authority	The fact that an authority takes a particular position on a certain issue is not in itself a sufficient guarantee that the argument holds. For example, if you take the same position as a scholar, this does not mean that you are exempted from further argumentation. You will have to explain why the expert takes this position.	This theory is correct (Author A, 2011).
The majority view	If many people, or the majority of a group of people, hold a particular opinion or take a particular position, this does not mean that it is right.	For example, even if the majority of the population thinks that parliamentary democracy is the best form of government, this is not indisputably true.
False links (spurious correlations)	The fact that two things are connected does not automatically mean that one follows from the other.	For example, if research shows that rich people are on average happier than poor people, you cannot conclude that money makes people happier. Other factors may be at play, and you could also argue it the other way around: it might be that someone's level of happiness influences their economic success.

▼

Logical fallacies	Conclusions or views that do not follow logically from the arguments that have been discussed.	For example, if a lot of research shows that disarming the Middle East would lead to peace, you cannot conclude from this that if there is no disarmament, there will certainly be no peace. There are also other ways of achieving peace.
Reversing the burden of proof	When you claim something, you should be the one to assume the burden of proof for your claim. Saying that someone else should prove the opposite of your claims is misleading and does not substantiate your own view.	For example: 'Why *does* God exist? You prove that God *doesn't* exist.'
False opposition	Two opposing options are advanced, while there are in fact many more.	For example: 'What would you rather see covered by medical insurance: Viagra pills for macho men or at-home care for old grannies?'
The slippery slope	Insinuating that an intervention or measure will take things from bad to worse, while it is far from guaranteed that it will have this effect.	For example: 'If we include Viagra in the basic package for medical insurance today, then tomorrow we'll be reimbursing breast enlargements.'

The structure of a scholarly article

A scholarly article reflects the continuous process of scholarship (see *Figure 1 on p. 13*), which is why the empirical cycle is reflected in the structure of scholarly articles. You discuss the theory (based on previous research) in the introduction to your article, the testing of the data in the middle section, and the conclusion and evaluation in the discussion section. This division is known as the **IMD structure** (Introduction – Middle section – Discussion). Exactly what is discussed in these three parts is dependent on your discipline, but some aspects are always present. We will address these in the following sections.

Figure 9.4 The empirical cycle. In general, previous research or the observation of a phenomenon leads to a theory, which can thus be seen as the start of the empirical cycle. Testing the data produces results, and these lead to a conclusion. This is evaluated, which in turn produces ideas for new research. And this brings us back to the beginning of the process again.

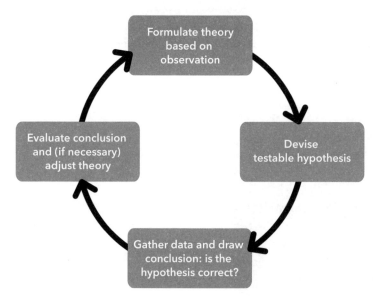

It can generally be said that the IMD structure is based on the **'hourglass model'**. This means that the content of the introduction and the conclusion is broad, whereas the content of the description in the middle section is specific and narrow. By 'broad content', we mean that the article begins and ends with general information. For example, this includes the definition used in your article for the concepts you employ. As you learned in *Chapter 4*, when doing research, you choose one or more dimensions that fit with your research question. This means that your report becomes substantively narrower, because you can only investigate part of the concept. In the discussion section, you again formulate the substantive findings more broadly and generally, so that you can nevertheless say something (cautiously) about the whole concept.

In the rest of this chapter, we first offer some tips on what you should address in the introduction, the middle section and the discussion. When it comes to the middle section, scholarly articles can be divided roughly into two groups. The difference between them lies in the way the research question is answered. In the case of a literature review or review article, the question is answered by searching the literature. What has been found about this subject and how do these research studies relate to one another? This means that you discuss and compare different articles, which allows you to answer the research question. With a research article, the research question is answered by gathering data using quantitative or qualitative methods (*Chapter 8*). As this has implications for the structure and content of the middle section (see *Figures 9.5A and 9.5B*), we discuss both here.

Figure 9.5A Schematic overview of the components of a literature review and how these are reflected in the hourglass model. The introduction consists of the theoretical framework, the problem statement, the research question, and the structure. In the middle section, the various relevant research studies are discussed and compared. The discussion consists of the conclusion, evaluation, limitations, suggestions for follow-up research, and the implications.

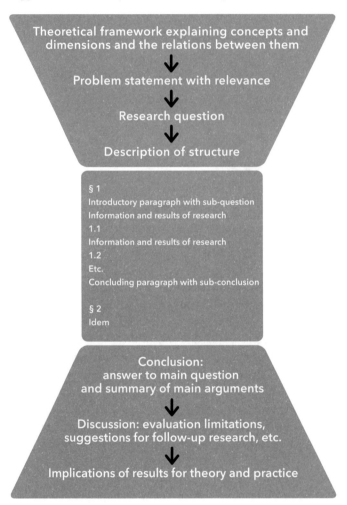

Figure 9.5B Schematic overview of the parts of a research article and how these are reflected in the hourglass model. The introduction consists of the theoretical framework, the problem statement, the research question, and the hypothesis, design, and predictions. The middle section consists of the materials and methods and the results. The discussion consists of the conclusion, evaluation, limitations, suggestions for follow-up research, and the implications. These parts are marked in the research article in Appendix B.

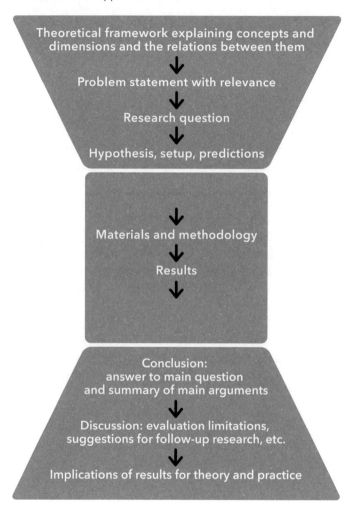

The introduction

In terms of content, the introduction starts broadly and becomes narrower (see *Figures 9.5A and 9.5B*). This means that your introduction begins with a broad, general introduction, with the definitions, and an explanation of the concepts that you're going to investigate. You also describe the potential relationship between these concepts (theoretical framework) and why investigating this relationship is relevant to society and/or scholarship (problem statement). This is explained in *Chapter 4*. Your research question (*Chapter 5*) thus follows logically from this. You substantiate all of this information based on the literature.

In some disciplines, it is common for this to be followed by a **hypothesis**: what answer can you expect to find, based on the literature? Finally, in many disciplines, it is common to provide a brief description of the **experimental setup**: what is your dependent variable, what is your independent variable, and which indicators are you going to use to test them? After the design section, you can conclude your introduction with a **prediction** or **expectation**, whereby you explain what you expect to come out of the variable.

The middle section

The literature review

Below, we explain how to write the middle section of your literature review. As a rule, a literature review is an article in which you describe the current state of the research in a certain field or in relation to a certain theme or problem. In doing so, you draw links between different scholarly sources and criticize them. In general, the main question consists of different sub-questions that are addressed in separate sections.

The middle section of the text is where you develop the question and use the information to answer the question. The middle section is the longest part of the text, and it is where the reader will find the lion's share of the argumentation on which the answer to the main question is based. In a literature review, you describe the experiments, results, and conclusions of various articles. In doing so, it is essential that you only report the information that is needed from the articles to answer your question. This is done in different sections.

In each section, you should answer one sub-question. A literature review should not be a collection of summaries. Thus, if you are drawing on three articles, you should not describe a different article in each section; on the contrary, it is important to link and integrate the different articles. This means that you should reflect beforehand on which subtopic you want to address in a section, and then take information from all of the studies that say something about this. The key thing is that you only select useful information. For example, you might be using an article in which three experiments are described. If only the first experiment is relevant to your question, then you should only describe the first experiment and say nothing about the other two.

Furthermore, the following factors are important for structuring the sections in the middle part:
- You should start each section with an **introductory paragraph** in which you explain why this subtopic is important for your main question. This allows you to make a transition from the previous section. By then formulating a sub-question (see also *Chapter 5*), you give direction to your section, so that the reader knows what you are going to investigate there.

- Then you report the information and results from other research studies that are relevant to answering the sub-question. When describing the research, you should not discuss everything in minute detail, but only data that are relevant to your subtopic.
- You need not wait until the end of your text (the conclusion/discussion) to evaluate the research. If your evaluation includes a critique of the research methodology, for example, it is more logical to put this straight after the description of the research in question. There should be a clear separation between the description of the research on the one hand, and the evaluation on the other hand. Ensure that you always make it clear where the information is coming from. If you take others' critical points on board, you should always cite the source. Usually, your own evaluation will be clear because the information is not accompanied by a citation, not because you've used the word 'I' (which should ideally be avoided).
- Every section should finish with a short **sub-conclusion**. In this, you should summarize the most important results and conclusions once more, and you should state how the (possibly contradictory) results can be explained. Here, you also give an explicit and detailed answer to the sub-question you addressed in this section. In addition, this paragraph would be a good place for specific evaluations of the research studies discussed.
- Ensure that every section has a heading and that the sections are linked effectively with good transitionary sentences. Adding well-chosen subheadings makes the literature review easier to follow. Pay attention both to the text of the section headings and to their place in the report. Choose short, substantive texts for the headings. An example of a good substantive heading is: 'The relationship between water footprint and cattle farming'. An example of a weak heading that lacks content is: 'The research by Barona et al. (2010)'.

The research article

In a research article, you answer the research question by gathering and analysing data. This means that the middle section is subdivided into a methodology section (also known as the 'materials and methods section') and a results section. In the **methodology section**, you describe how the research was carried out, so the results can be interpreted and the experiment can be replicated. In the **results section** , you describe what came out of your experiment. Both parts lie on the narrowest point of the hourglass model (*Figure 9.5B*).

Methodology

In order to ensure replicability, it is important to describe this part in sufficient detail. In order to keep things readable, though, it is essential to be as concise as possible. You should describe the factors that affected the results, but you can leave out anything that is obviously required to deliver reliable work. By way of comparison, think of a recipe in a cookbook. Quantities and actions are essential in a recipe, but it doesn't matter whether you mix the products in a mixing bowl or a pan.

Depending on the kind of research you're doing, the description is divided into different subheadings. Check out published articles that are similar to your research to see how to create a logical system of subheadings. Headings that almost always feature in such sections are the subjects of the research, the procedure and the (statistical) analysis.

Under **subjects of research**, you describe the subjects in the broadest sense. These could be a plant species, animal test subjects, a population of human test subjects, or a microbiological cell line, but also, for example, your respondents. You report all of the details of the test subjects or human test subjects you used in the research, such as their gender, age and origin. You should also mention all of the conditions the research subjects had to meet (inclusion criteria) or not (exclusion criteria) during the recruitment. Describe the sample size, the sampling method, and how the research subjects were divided into groups (see *Chapter 7*).

In the **procedure** section, the research design is described in full and in detail, often in chronological order. By providing a good, comprehensive description of the procedure, you show that you have reflected carefully on the methodology of the research, taking account of controls, randomization, and any potential confounding factors. In the **analysis** you describe what you did with your data. For example, which statistical test(s) you used to compare the impact of the independent variable(s) on the dependent variable(s). In addition, you should mention the analysis program that you used here (such as SPSS or R, including the version number).

Results

The results section, like the materials and methods section, lies on the narrowest point of the hourglass model. This means that you are not concerned with the concepts or dimensions that you are researching, only with the indicators and their outcome measures. You describe the most important findings of the research as objectively as you can. Therefore, in natural scientific research, it is important not to do any interpretation here. Interpreting, explaining, and concluding on the basis of these results should be saved for the discussion section.

Note that this rule of thumb does not always apply. In some disciplines, it is actually important to interpret here, because this forms part of your result. When conducting semi-structured interviews, for example, the answers are described, but an important part of the results is a separate analysis section that gives an interpretation of the results (*Chapter 8*). You should therefore always ask your lecturer what you are meant to do.

If applicable, it is common to start the results section by reporting if any research subjects have dropped out and the reason for this. If you are doing quantitative research, you will be making use of statistics to test your hypothesis. In that case, you will write the results in the running text, placing statistical values in brackets at the end of the sentence. You should always describe the direction of the statistical difference: more/less/higher/lower/better/worse.

For every result, you should give a verbal description of the research result, substantiated with descriptive statistics and comparative (testing) statistics. For all of the different statistical tests, you should describe the sample size, the number of measures of freedom, and the p-value. For example, you might write: 'Per match, significantly more points were scored by volleyball players who train twice a week ($M = 22.3$, $SD = 3.4$) than by those who train once a week ($M = 16.2$, $SD = 4.6$, $t(61) = 5.12$, $p < 0.05$).' It is wise to consult a statistics textbook or your lecturer on how to present the statistical tests, as each scholarly journal has different formatting conventions (just as citation formats can differ). The format that we use here is that used by the American Psychological Association (APA).

Ensure that the most important results are also displayed in a figure, or possibly in a table. You should only use relevant data. Other data that support your research, but that are not essential to your story, can be put in an appendix. There are many options for presenting your data. Think about what you want to present: what do you want your readers to see at a glance? If you want to show a trend over time, for example, a line chart is a good option, but if you are concerned with the difference between two or more groups, then a box plot or bar chart will probably convey the main issue more effectively. A table can be a good way of giving an overview of your results.

Note that a figure or table should never be the only place where your data are presented: they should also be included in the text! A figure or table should be comprehensible in itself for the reader, so the caption (figure) or heading (table) should contain enough detail for this. Finally, don't forget to refer to your figures and tables in the text. In *Box 9.2* you will find extra advice, tips, and conditions for presenting your data.

Figures

In a **figure**, it is common to display descriptive statistics (for example, average and standard deviation) and to use symbols to indicate significant effects. The latter is usually done by inserting an asterisk. Keep it visually simple:

- Don't use colours or shading in the background.
- Shading should only be used occasionally for very complex tables with lots of cells, and you should only use light grey.
- Don't use 3D (unless this is common in your field and data cannot be displayed in any other way) or icons (for example, piglets to represent meat production). The latter imply a certain interpretation of the data, something you want to avoid

Table

A **table** can be a good way of presenting a quantity of data in a structured way. Like figures, there are also rules of thumb for formatting tables. For example, if you are using APA formatting, you should only make the horizontal lines of the table visible, and the significant values should be indicated with an asterisk. You should ask your lecturer which convention to follow. It is always important to round off numbers to a relevant value. Averages or total sums are always put underneath a table or at the end of a row, and never above it or on the left-hand side.

Box 9.2   *Rules for captions for figures and tables (Booth et al., 2008)*

Rule	Example
Make a clear distinction between captions for tables and for figures. Don't forget to refer to figures or tables in the text, either.	A **table** has a title; this should be put above the table, aligned left. A **figure** has a legend; this should be put under the figure, aligned left.
Do not make the caption overly general.	Not: 'Water use' but: 'Change in water consumption for meat production between 2000 and 2010'.
Don't be too sparing with your use of labels. This is particularly important if you want to distinguish between different graphical representations of similar-looking data.	Thus, not one label with: 'Water use, meat production', but separate labels for: 'Change in water consumption for meat production in France, 2000-2010', and 'Change in water consumption for meat production in Spain, 2002-2015'.

The discussion and the conclusion

You will use your results to draw a conclusion. In some disciplines, the conclusion usually falls under a separate heading; in others, the conclusion falls under the heading of the discussion section. Whatever the case, this final section of your report follows the shape of the bottom section of the hourglass. In a mirror image of the introduction, you start specifically (narrow), based on the research findings, and during the discussion the measurable variables are translated back into substantively broad concepts. Common elements in the discussion are a conclusion, evaluation, suggestions for follow-up research, limitations of the study, and implications.

It is common to start your **discussion** with a short summary of the most important results, and draw one overarching **conclusion** from this that directly answers the research question (and sub-questions). Here you should only discuss the results that are already described in the middle section. Subsequently, you are going to **evaluate** this conclusion. You can do this by going back to the theoretical framework that you described in the introduction. Does this conclusion support the theory? Why does/ doesn't it? Or which part of the theory does it support and which part does it not support? Are there other studies that have the same findings as yours? And studies that found something different? How can this be? In doing so, don't forget to cite the literature.

As you can see, there are many options, which means the structure of the discussion section is less rigid than, say, that of the introduction. Regardless of your conclusion and the direction of your evaluation, you will probably identify starting points for **follow-up research**. It is common to describe these: in doing so, you complete the empirical cycle, as they count as new observations. Consider the following:

- What research questions are raised by your results?
- What would you do differently if you were to research the topic again? How could you overcome the limitations (see below)?
- In what other context could you investigate the relationship between the concepts?

Another part that often features in a discussion section is a description of the **limitations** of the study. These are those things that could have affected your outcome measure. You do not know this for sure, of course, but if earlier articles have shown that a certain factor (for example, male-female differences) could have had an impact and you failed to take this into account, it is important to mention this. It is extremely important to be transparent, because this is information the reader needs in order to be able to assess the value of your results (see also *Chapter 9*).

In addition, as a researcher, you will have considered many factors that needed to be overcome as effectively as possible. For example, factors that could be influenced in advance, such as setting up your design, or afterwards, such as carrying out an extra control analysis. Describing what you did to overcome the limitations as effectively as possible strengthens your story, because it shows the reader that you have thought about it carefully. In any case, it is standard to link these limitations to suggestions for follow-up research, and thus give an initial impulse to solving them.

The last part that often features is the **implications** of your study. In this part, you return to your problem statement, in which you described how researching this relationship is relevant to society and/or scholarship. What does the present research contribute? What problem have you solved (or failed to solve) with this conclusion? Here, too, it is important to refer to the literature. Ensure that you always conclude with a strong last sentence, such as the main conclusion of your research.

Valorization

Recently, there has been increasing emphasis on **valorization**; politicians highlight its importance and researchers are increasingly being asked how their research results can be valorized. Valorization can be seen as a process of creating social value from knowledge, for example by transforming this knowledge into products, services, processes, and new enterprises (Wakkee, Lips, Löwik, Wijnen, Schöller, n.d.).

Valorization is thus a process, which means that scientists do not simply explain how their findings can contribute to a social or economic application, as is sometimes the case in the discussion section of a scholarly article; instead, they interact with other parties (outside the university) to add value to 'pure' scientific results. For example, if a research study shows that a certain intervention is valuable for patients, then in order to valorize these results, scientists can establish a partnership with hospital support staff, patients, therapists, and health insurers, in order to develop a tailor-made solution in the hospital.

In order to ensure that your scholarly research and knowledge contribute to a social goal, you can go through the different steps of the valorization process. Below, we address the first two steps (based on Wakkee et al., n.d.), which can help you to start talking to other parties (outside the university).

1 Think about who could benefit from your findings.
2 These contacts can be a relatively easy way to start a dialogue and find out about the most recent developments in practice – and the extent to which your results connect with these.
3 Make your idea specific.
4 You can make your idea more specific by asking the following questions: What is the idea? What problem or issue does it solve? Who benefits from this solution? What is the advantage of your solution compared to existing solutions?

Most knowledge institutions have a separate department that is responsible for valorization and brings together social parties and scholars. You should therefore find out what's available at the organization where you're studying or doing an internship.

Sources

Booth, W.C., Colomb, G.G., & Williams, J.M. (2008). *The Craft of Research, third edition*. Chicago: University of Chicago Press.

Kahn, J. (n.d.). Reporting statistics in APA style. Retrieved from https://my.ilstu.edu/~jhkahn/apastats.html

Toulmin, S.E. (2003). *The Uses of Argument, Updated Edition*. Cambridge: Cambridge University Press.

Wakkee, I., Lips, F., Löwik, S., Wijnen, A., & Schöller, D. (n.d.). *IXA Valorisation guide - Practical handbook for social sciences and humanities researchers* [pdf]. Amsterdam: AIX.

10 Finishing your article: academic writing, titles, and abstracts

From a substantive perspective, your story is now complete. You've written the introduction, the materials and methods section, the results, and the discussion. The last important elements of a research article are the title and the abstract. And when you finish, it is important to check your article for clarity, brevity, writing style, consistency, and spelling. In short, in order to be able to write a good article, you also need to know the requirements for academic writing.

The title and the abstract

The **title** of a research article should be informative and written as a fluent sentence, so that it clearly communicates the key conclusion of the report. You may want to elucidate the main title with a subtitle. The **abstract** of an article is often to be found on the article's cover page. It is the text that is shown in a search engine and is always freely accessible. For this reason, it is important that it contains a brief summary of all parts of the report, and enough information to allow it to be read and understood independently of the article. An abstract is often written as a standalone summary, with each part that is described following on logically from the last. Usually, it is the only part of a scientific text that doesn't contain any references. See *Box 10.1* for a checklist on what should be included in an abstract.

Box 10.1   Checklist abstract

Checklist for the abstract

1 The aim of the research study (the problem statement and research question).
2 The methods that were used to answer the research question.
3 The results.
4 The conclusions that were drawn and their relevance.

Writing clearly

Scholarly articles tend to be difficult to read, and this certainly hasn't improved over the last thirty years (Knight, 2003). This has to do with the emergence of new academic sub-disciplines with their own jargon, but also the fact that few scholars are trained to **write clearly**. This is a problem, because as a writer, you need to get your message across to the reader. If your writing is unclear, readers will interpret it in their own way, and you, the writer, will no longer have any influence over their interpretation. As a result, you won't know whether you've got your message across.

Gopen and Swan (1990) investigated how the readability of an article could be improved without simplifying the content. The following tips are based on their research, as well as that of Knight (2003):

- Avoid **discontinuous structures**. These are sentence constructions that leave a lot of space between related phrases. Not: 'A man walked by wearing a hat,' But: 'A man wearing a hat walked by.'
- The last part of the sentence is the **stress position** or **topic position**. In other words, the reader will remember the information that is placed there – so this is where you should put the most important information. For example, if you write: 'Sales rose after the product ingredients were altered,' the emphasis is on the change to the product; but if you write, 'After the product ingredients were altered, sales rose', the emphasis is on the rise in sales.
- The first part of a sentence is the part the reader needs in order to understand the logical progression of the text. By this, the authors mean that you, the writer, must begin a sentence by building progressively on the information in the previous sentence. You can do this with repetition, for example. If you fail to do this, the reader has to make a mental leap. Not all readers will do this, meaning that you won't communicate your message effectively.
  - You can also use linking sentences and signal words to connect paragraphs and sentences together. See *Box 3.1* for a list of signal words and their role in a text.
- Make effective use of verbs, as they indicate the actions that are taking place. By this, for instance, it is meant that you should avoid writing: 'We are making an effort to achieve an improvement in our position', but instead write: 'We are endeavouring to improve our position.' In a long sentence, the reader uses verbs as a crutch; using verbs that impart something about the content adds structure to the sentence
  - Avoid using the passive voice wherever possible. The passive voice makes a text come across as impersonal and non-active. For example: 'People were advised by the police to stay inside.' You can make this more active: 'The police advised people to stay inside.' One tip here is that after writing a text, you should go through it and replace as many passive constructions as you can with active ones.
  - Note that one exception to this is active sentences containing personal pronouns (I, you, he, she, etc.). This is because in academic texts, it doesn't matter who did something, but *that* something was done. The passive form: 'The statistical test was subsequently carried out', is therefore better than the active form: 'I subsequently carried out a statistical test.'

Academic language use

In addition to the general tips above, the genre of 'academic writing' also has its own characteristic style. If you ask what this style is, many students will say that it revolves around the use of professional language and the avoidance of popular language. This is true, of course (your text deserves a serious tone), but there are two other aspects that are more important.

In academic writing, everything revolves around clarity, first and foremost. After all, the research should be verifiable and replicable. A second important characteristic is succinctness, as many scholarly journals have strict word limits. You may feel that it is an art to balance these two: ensuring that you describe everything in your article clearly, without using too many words. This is a skill that requires practice.

For this reason, keep looking critically at your text and remember to 'kill your darlings'. To achieve brevity, it is important to remove unnecessary digressions or subordinate clauses. In order to improve the clarity of your text, there are things you can bear in mind:

- Be accurate in your descriptions: The sentence: 'The Dutch changed energy supplier much more often in 2013', is missing important information. For example, it is not clear with whom the Dutch are being compared and precisely what 'much more often' means. It would be better to write: 'The Dutch changed energy supplier twice as often in 2013 than in the previous year.'
- Be nuanced in your claims: your text should imply that your claims are not irrefutably true, and you should leave space for new, possibly better insights that might arise in future.
- Avoid ambiguity: even if a sentence is grammatically correct, it may not be clear. For example, the sentence 'Mark saw a girl looking out of the window of the room' can give rise to misunderstandings on the reader's part: is Mark or the girl looking out of the window?
- Use demonstrative pronouns carefully: when referring back to a previous sentence (for example, when using the demonstrative pronouns 'this', 'that', and 'those'), make sure that it is absolutely clear to what you are referring. Don't make your reader search for the meaning, as this will detract from your argument.
- Avoid abbreviations: Don't use 'e.g.' and 'i.e.', but 'for example' and 'that is to say'. Abbreviations of institutions' names may be used if written out in full on first use, with the abbreviation given in brackets. One exception is 'et al.' which is an abbreviation for 'et alii' ('and others' in Latin), which is used in references.
- Finally, check your report carefully for minor errors that can detract from the content; see the checklist in *Box 10.2*.

Box 10.2 Checklist: once you've finished writing, check your report for:

Spelling and style errors	These errors detract from the point the writer wants to make. The fact that there are spelling errors suggests that other things are wrong, too. Pay particular attention to: • Grammatical and spelling errors. • Apostrophes, especially possessives. 'It's' is the short form of 'it is' or 'it has'. • Correct notation of numbers and symbols. Numbers under twenty should be written out wherever possible; chemical elements and formulas should be written correctly (CO_2 and not CO2). • Fewer and less. 'Fewer' should be used for items that can be counted individually (count nouns), whereas 'less' should be used for things that cannot be counted individually (mass nouns). Fewer: 'Ten books or fewer.' Less: 'The presentation should take less time.' • Which or that. Use 'that' when the added information is crucial to understanding the sentence. Use 'which' when the added information is not crucial to understanding the sentence. If you use 'which', make sure you offset the added information with commas. That: 'Foods that contain sugar are the worst.' Which: 'The pasta in the canteen, which contained several kinds of vegetables, was a healthy option.'
Sentence length	It is generally the case that the more subordinate clauses there are in a sentence, the less clear it becomes.
Paragraph use	Be consistent with your formatting: paragraphs should be separated by a line or indented with a tab. Ensure that your paragraphs are neither too long nor too short. A rule of thumb: a paragraph should contain between three and ten sentences.
Don't use exclamation marks	Let your arguments speak for themselves.
References (see Chapter 11)	• Every statement you make should be accompanied by a citation. • Every citation in the text should be accompanied by a reference in the bibliography. • Every article in the bibliography should be accompanied by a citation in the text. If you have not cited an article in the text, then it shouldn't be in the bibliography.
Formatting	Take a careful look at the formatting of the references, figures and statistical values. Ensure that you've been consistent and have used the same style throughout (number of decimals, etc.).

Sources

Gopen, G.D., & Swan, J.A. (1990). The science of scientific writing, *American Scientist, 78*, 550-558.

Knight, J. (2003). Clear as mud. *Nature, 423*, 376-378.

Oost, H., & Markenhof, A. (2002). *Een onderzoek rapporteren*. Baarn: HB uitgevers.

Renkema, J. (2005). *Schrijfwijzer*. The Hague: Sdu Uitgevers.

Other useful sources

At the website of the University of Toronto, you'll find some more tips on academic writing: writing.utoronto.ca/advice

Various websites offer advice on technical language issues, such as spelling and word use: www.oxforddictionaries.com, www.oed.com.

The book *Effective writing in English* by M. Hannay and J. Lachlan Mackenzie (2002) is a comprehensive book that aims to give writers more control over their texts.

The book *English grammar in use* by Raymond Murphy (2015) is aimed at non-native speakers of English who need to write in English. It describes key points of grammar and syntax for students.

11 Citing sources and the bibliography

Citing sources is something that's done in every academic text: partly to indicate the status quo in the research field, but mainly so that you can substantiate your argument with others' views and research. It is very important to do this with great precision, and in this chapter, you will learn when and how to use citations in your work.

Making effective use of citations in your interdisciplinary text will increase the chance of your work being taken seriously by scholars from different academic disciplines. Citation has various functions:

- To acknowledge work by other researchers. Failing to cite others' work or citing it incorrectly when the work has been used in the content of the text constitutes **plagiarism** (see *Chapter 12*). In any case, the reader should know exactly when you are expressing your own ideas (for example, in the form of criticism, a conclusion, or an appraisal) and when you're quoting others.
- To anchor your own text in the context of different disciplines. If you don't link your text explicitly to what's currently happening in the research field, you'll soon be considered uninformed.
- To substantiate your own claims; sources then function like arguments with verification. You thereby give the reader an opportunity to check your claims and further investigate an idea from your work.

As you write, you will mostly use information from texts written by others. You can use this information in your report in two ways. First, you can **quote**; that is, literally copy excerpts of text written by others. As well as text, this could be diagrams, images, or tables. Second, you can **paraphrase**; that is, reproduce others' ideas and information in your own words. Whether you choose to quote or paraphrase depends on the kind of text that you're writing and on the role the passage to be cited or paraphrased plays in your text. Resist the temptation to overload your text with quotes. You should only quote when strictly necessary, such as when the source text expresses an idea, insight, or argument so beautifully that paraphrasing would fail to do justice to it..

Commonly acknowledged sources do not need to be cited. For example, the statement that 'water boils at 100 °C or 212 °F' does not need to be backed up with a citation. During your studies, you will gradually develop a feeling for the kind of information that can be assumed to be common knowledge within different disciplines. As you get more experienced at reading scholarly texts, it will become easier to make this choice: you will get better at spotting the ways in which professional scholars in your discipline cite sources.

Thus, in your literature survey, try to state as accurately as possible where you got the information. This is done in the running text, immediately after the information that you have taken from the source and included in your own report. In addition, at the end of your report, provide a detailed overview of all the sources you have used in a reference list or bibliography.

In academia, there are different standards for formatting references, and they are different for each discipline and sub-discipline. If you are looking for examples in scholarly journals, you will see that the citation methods are often different. This is because every journal chooses its own reference style. The most common reference styles can be found in *Box 11.1*. One widely used reference style is APA style, and we will explain this form of citation further here.

Box 11.1   Citation methods

Citation method	Organization	Website
APA	American Psychological Association	www.apastyle.org
CSE	Council of Science Editors	www.cbe.org
CMS	Chicago Manual of Style	www.chicagomanualofstyle.org
MLA	Modern Language Association	www.mla.org

Reference management software

Many researchers use **reference management software**, which automatically puts the citation in the text and the reference in the bibliography in the right format. This can save you a lot of time and spare you many errors. A licence is often needed for this software, so you should check with your university or college library to see which reference management software packages your institution has a licence for.

In general, reference management programs have the following functions:

- They provide a central place where you can save all of the literature you're using and the accompanying PDF files. This allows you to categorize, search, and comment on articles, and you'll never mislay an article.
- They often allow you to make an automatic bibliography in every possible citation style. This means that you can be sure that you are using the correct citation style.
- They allow you to insert direct citations in Word (or another word-processing program) in your choice of style. You can subsequently generate a bibliography containing all of the literature you've used.

Switching from typing bibliographies by hand to a software package often requires a small investment in time (you have to find out how the program works), but it will make your life much easier, certainly later in your studies. One of the most popular – and the most user-friendly – programs is Mendeley.

Box 11.2 *Citation software*

In addition to Mendeley, there are also other reference management programs:	
ReadCube	This software largely has the same functionality as Mendeley. One advantage of this software is that you can also read articles from the program.
RefWorks	You manage your 'library' of citations online, so you always have it to hand. Many people do not consider this the most user-friendly program, however. What's more, you need a paid licence; access may be possible through your university. One advantage of RefWorks is that it is compatible with Windows PCs and Macs.
EndNote	The oldest and probably the best known of all the packages, but quite expensive and no longer the most useful. Can do pretty much the same things as the packages above.
BibTeX	This is not really reference management software as such, but the language and software that you use in combination with LaTeX – the system used by many scientists to write and format their articles. Some of the above-mentioned packages (Mendeley, for example) can help you to make BibTeX files.
Word	Versions of Word from Word 2007 onwards allow you to enter citations by hand and automatically generate a bibliography in the correct format. You can find this option under the 'References' tab.

Mendeley is a relatively new, free package that also saves your library online. It has a number of advantages in comparison to other software packages: (1) it is free, (2) it is user-friendly, (3) you can create references by dragging a PDF file into the program (it automatically extracts the author, title, year, etc.), (4) you can create references by using a browser plug-in to click on a button on the page where you found an article, (5) you can share articles and reference lists with colleagues, and (6) it has a 'web importer' to add sources rapidly to your own list.

In-text citations

Below, we have listed the most important ways to cite in the text following APA style.

Quotes

A number of standard rules apply to literal quotes.

- A quote must be copied exactly from the source, including capital letters, punctuation marks, and (possibly incorrect) spelling.
- Never include a quote in your text without an explanation. Ensure a good link between the quote and the text.
- Put parentheses after the quote: the author, the year of publication, and the page numbers. Then end the sentence with a full stop. If the publication has already been mentioned in the lead-up to the quote, just mentioning the page number(s) will be sufficient.
- If you leave out part of the quote, you should indicate this with three interspaced dots.
- Should you want to add something to the quote for clarification, put your comments in square brackets.

A short quote of fewer than forty words can simply be included in the text. In this case, the quote should be put after a colon and between quotation marks. For example:

In his research, Fearnside (2000) states the following: 'Soybeans represent a recent and powerful threat to biodiversity in Brazil' (p. 23).

Should the quote be longer than forty words, leave a blank line before and after the quote and indent the text. In this case, you do not need to put the quote in quotation marks. For example:

Once you've chosen a research topic, before finalizing it, it's best to make an inventory of the context of the topic. ... [The best way is to] search for angles onto your topic and [to] look at which ones are described. ... You might choose to connect your research to existing research and you can further specify your research topic (Plooij, 2011, p. 53).

Paraphrasing

Paraphrasing is a good way to incorporate information from a source in your own argument. Ensure that you do not reproduce the text of the source too literally, but that you summarize the essence of the text in your own words and cite the source. According to APA rules, a source citation in the text of a scholarly article consists of the name or names of the author(s) and the year. See *Box 11.3* for key considerations when formatting citations. You can refer to scholarly literature in a number of ways using APA style.

1 Only the year in parentheses:

'Research by Fearnside (2000) shows that soil degradation is a significant problem in Brazil.'

2 Authors' names *and* year in parentheses:

'Research shows that soil degradation is a significant problem in Brazil (Fearnside, 2000).'

3 Indirect reference to a source:

Should you refer several times to the same source within the same section, it is not always necessary to put a citation at the end of every paraphrased sentence, so long as the text shows the source of the information.

'Research by Fearnside (2000) shows that soil degradation is a significant problem in Brazil. ... This research also shows that...'

4 Unknown authors:

If you want to refer to a source written by an unknown author, something that often happens when citing research reports, refer to the first words of the reference as it is given in the bibliography (often the title) and the year of publication:

First citation: 'This report showed that... (Food and Agriculture Organization [FAO], 2013)', or: 'The report by the Food and Agriculture Organization (FAO; 2013) showed that...'

With subsequent in-text citations, you can use the abbreviation: '(FAO, 2013)' or 'FAO (2013)'.

5 If you have not read a publication yourself:

First of all, you should only cite literature that you have read. If you come across a reference in a publication to another publication that you also want to use, it is best to track down this publication and read it. If this is not possible, refer to the publication via the other publication you've found. In this way, for example, you avoid the possibility of indiscriminately reproducing dubious or incorrect interpretations. Nor should you include the publication that you've cited indirectly in the bibliography. An example from *Appendix A:* 'In their book People of the tropical rain forest, Denslow and Padoch (1988, cited in Baroni et al., 2007) show that ...'

Box 11.3   Checklist for in-text citations

Citation element	Explanation	Example
initials	Authors' initials or first names are never included in in-text citations, but they are included in the bibliography at the end of the paper.	The research by Marcia L. Spetch and Donald M. Wilkie as a citation: (Spetch & Wilkie, 1983)
'and' and '&'	If the names are not in brackets, the word 'and' is used; if the names are in brackets, the sign '&' is used.	According to Christopherson and Birkeland (2013), it seems likely that... (Christopherson & Birkeland, 2013)
full stop	The citation is part of the sentence and therefore comes before the full stop.	For sufficient ... (Christopherson & Birkeland, 2013).
et al. (multiple authors)	For publications by six or more authors, you can generally use the short form of the citation. The short form consists of the name of the first author followed by the addition 'et al.' (abbreviation for: 'et alii', Latin for 'and others') and the year. If a publication has three to five authors, all the authors' names are given in the first citation, and the short form can be used in later citations.	Baroni et al. (2007) investigated the ... Or: ... an important source of eutrophication (Foster et al., 2006). First citation: In the research by Ercin, Aldaya, and Hoekstra (2012), ... Or: ... (Ercin, Aldaya & Hoekstra, 2012). Thereafter: Ercin et al. (2012) investigated the ...

Citations in the bibliography

At the end of a paper or research article, you provide an overview of all of the sources that you cited in the text. This should only include the sources that you have read; articles that you have not read or did not use in the text do not need to be included. In any case, every reference contains the following elements: the authors, year of publication, title, and location (for example, the name of a scholarly journal). The most common options are listed here, but you can consult www.apastyle.org for a complete overview. Here, you will learn how to cite a chapter from a multi-author volume, doctoral and Master's theses, newspaper articles, and films, among other things.

Some general rules to keep in mind:
- The list should be in alphabetical order, by the surname of the first author.
- You should use indentations to distinguish the different references from each other (don't use bullet points).
- Digital articles often have a Digital Object Identifier (DOI). This is a unique identification number and a permanent link to the location of the digital source. This permanent link is constructed as follows: https://doi.org/ [doi-identificationnumber]
- Prefixes in names, such as 'van', 'van der', etc., should be placed after the author's initial or initials (see the first example of referencing under books in the following section).
- If the author is unknown, you should refer to the organization. If the organization is also unknown, you should give the title of the web page.
- Note that when citing scholarly journals, volume numbers are known as 'issues'.

Journals

The following formatting should be used for articles from scholarly journals:

General format – digital version with DOI:

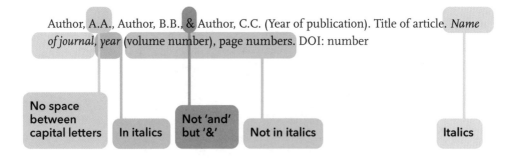

Author, A.A., Author, B.B., & Author, C.C. (Year of publication). Title of article. *Name of journal, year* (volume number), page numbers. DOI: number

No space between capital letters

In italics

Not 'and' but '&'

Not in italics

Italics

Paper version:
Author, A.A., Author, B.B., & Author, C.C. (Year of publication). Title of article. *Name of journal, year* (volume number), page numbers.

Example – 1 author
Mellers, B.A. (2000). Choice and the relative pleasure of consequences. *Psychological Bulletin, 126,* 910-924. doi: http://doi.org/10.1037/0033-2909.126.6.910

Example – 2 authors
Klimoski, R., & Palmer, S. (1993). The ADA and the hiring process in organizations. *Consulting Psychology Journal: Practice and Research, 45*(2), 10-36. doi: http://doi.org/10.1037/1061-4087.45.2.10

Example – 3 to 5 authors (paper version)
Borman, W.C., Hanson, M.A., Oppler, S.H., Pulakos, E.D., & White, L.A. (1993). Role of early supervisory experience in supervisor performance. *Journal of Applied Psychology, 78*, 443-449.

Example – more than 5 authors (paper version)
Wolchnik, S.A., West, S.G., Sandler, I.N., Tein, J., Coatsworth, D., Lengua, L., et al. (2000). An experimental evaluation of theory-based mother and mother-child programs for children of divorce. *Journal of Consulting and Clinical Psychology, 68*, 843-856.

Books

Paper version:

Author, A.A., Author, B.B., & Author, C.C. (Year of publication). *Title: Subtitle.* Place: Publisher.

No space between capital letters

In italics

Digital version:
Author, A.A., Author, B.B., & Author, C.C. (Year of publication). *Title: Subtitle.* Retrieved from http://url

Example – 2 authors (paper version)
Swales, J.M. & Feak, C.B. (2010). *Academic writing for graduate students: Essential tasks and skills (3ʳᵈ ed.).* Ann Arbor, MI: University of Michigan Press.

Example – 2 authors (digital version)
Dvorak, R., & Ferraz-Mello, S. (2005). *A comparison of the dynamical evolution of planetary systems.* doi: http://doi.org/doi:10.1007/1-4020-4466-6

Example – digital book without DOI and without publication year (n.d.: no date)
Rosenbaur, O. (n.d.). *Four realities.* Retrieved from http://www.onlineoriginals.com/showitem.asp?itemID=149.

Research reports

Author, A.A. (year). Title and subtitle (report number if available). Location: Publisher.

Colon

Author, A.A. (year). *Title and subtitle* (report number if available). Retrieved on day/month from http://url

Example – organization as author
Australian Bureau of Statistics (1991). *Estimated resident population by age and sex in statistical local areas, New South Wales* (3209.1). Canberra: Australian Capital Territory.

Example – digital book with organization as author
TransCanada (2018). *Annual report*. Retrieved on 16 May 2019 from https://www.transcanada.com/globalassets/pdfs/investors/transcanada-annual-report.pdf

Internet resources

Author, A.A. (year, day and month, if available). *Title of document*. Retrieved on day/month/year from http://url

Example – 3 authors
De Vos, E., WidPortier, C.J., & Leonard, W.L. (2016, 13 June). *Do cell phones cause cancer? Probably, but it's complicated*. Retrieved on 16 June 2016 from http://blogs.scientificamerican.com/guest-blog/do-cell-phones-cause-cancer-probably-but-it-s-complicated/

Example – Organization as author and without date (n.d.)
Institute for Interdisciplinary Studies (n.d.). Interdisciplinary education. Retrieved on 16 June 2016 from http://iis.uva.nl/en/interdisciplinary-education

Personal communication and interviews

If you've conducted an interview or spoken to someone, this does not count as publicly available data, and you should not include this as a source in your bibliography. However, you can cite the interview or the information that you were given by this person in the text as personal communication. For example: (A.A. Interviewee, personal communication, 11 March 2018).

In order to refer to an interview that is publicly available (for example, on a website), you should use the following format:

Interviewee, A.A. (year, day month). Title of interview. (A.A. Interviewer, interviewer). Title of web page. Retrieved from http://url

Example – interview

Kahneman, D. (2019, 13 March). The Map of Misunderstanding (S. Harris, interviewer). Making Sense with Sam Harris. Retrieved from https://samharris.org/podcasts/150-map-misunderstanding/

Sources

Poelmans, P., & Severijnen, O. (2014). *De APA-richtlijnen: Over literatuurverwijzingen en onderzoeksrapportage.* Bussum: Uitgeverij Coutinho.

University of Amsterdam (2014, 3 January). *Fraud and plagiarism* Retrieved from http://student.uva.nl/en/content/az/plagiarism-and-fraud/plagiarism-and-fraud.html

Other useful sources

At the APA website, you can find even more detailed advice on citations: apastyle.org. You can also find advice on APA's Facebook page: facebook.com/APAStyle.

12 Preventing fraud and plagiarism

Fraud and plagiarism should always be prevented. Unfortunately, it still sometimes happens that after publishing or submitting a text, one or more authors are caught for fraud or plagiarism.

By **plagiarism**, we mean copying ideas, passages, or words and presenting them as your own work. It is thus essential that you cite your sources well. By **fraud**, we mean the falsification of data. In the case of student assignments, plagiarism – and occasionally even fraud – are sometimes detected, too. In such cases, appeals to ignorance ('I didn't know that it was plagiarism') are rarely accepted as valid reasons for letting the perpetrator off the hook. Below, we set out some ways to check for plagiarism and fraud.

Plagiarism of written work

Here the art is to distinguish between those things for which you should credit someone and those things that are obvious and considered common knowledge. In the beginning, you will often have doubts, and in this case, you should play it safe. It is better to cite too many sources than too few. With more experience in reading scientific texts, it will become easier to make the call; you will develop a better eye for the way in which professional scholars in your field cite sources.

Sometimes it is difficult to figure out whether an idea really is your own or someone else's, and having a careful note-taking system will help with this. If you make notes as you read, write down what you've quoted literally (using quote marks) and note the publication and the page number where you found the quote you're copying or paraphrasing (see 'making a literature matrix', *Chapter 2*). This way, you won't be in for any nasty surprises when you've handed in your paper. A sloppy note-taking system is one of the main causes of plagiarism among students.

Plagiarism of fellow students

As a scholar, you never work in a vacuum. It is important to exchange ideas with others on the topics you're addressing. However, it is also important for your degree course that you learn to read and incorporate the material by yourself, so that you can then express your ideas in your own words. If work isn't done individually, lecturers cannot gauge the extent to which students have these skills and knowledge. For this reason, assignments that are not done individually – with the exception of group assignments – are also considered to be plagiarism, and there are penalties for this.

Both the perpetrator and the co-perpetrator of fraud and plagiarism can be penalized. If the work of a fellow student is copied with the permission or cooperation of the same student, then they are also complicit in the plagiarism. Sending assignments, papers, or other forms of work to fellow students can thus result in a penalty.

When plagiarism is committed by one of the authors of a group assignment, the other authors are also complicit in the plagiarism if they could or should have known that their fellow student was committing plagiarism. This means that a group is collectively responsible for the content of a piece of work. You should thus ensure as a group that you are involved in each other's research. Always read your fellow students' work carefully and point out where citations are missing, so that they can be looked up and added before the work is handed in.

Working responsibly in a team

As an academic, you learn to work in a team. Part of this entails taking responsibility for yourself and contributing in a reasonable way to the group work and group process. 'Free-riding' means participating in a group assignment but not contributing or contributing very little, such as by not turning up to group meetings, not preparing the work, or failing to meet prior agreements. In short: a free-rider shirks his or her responsibilities and attempts to pass a course with the minimum possible effort. Be sure to take part actively and know what is expected of you, and also ensure that the others know what is expected of them (see the team charter in *Chapter 13* for key tips). By using the team charter as a group, it is possible to prevent free-riding.

Nevertheless, if someone is free-riding and talking to them makes no difference, report this to your lecturer. Bear in mind that if you do this too late, your lecturer won't necessarily be able to do very much about it. In addition, it is difficult for a lecturer to weigh everything up if it's your word against the free-rider's. Thus, always ensure that you document the meetings and appointments well, so you can go back to what has been promised and see which agreements have not been met (see also *Chapter 13*).

Fraud: falsifying data

It is absolutely out of the question to falsify data in order to boost your research findings. But in some cases, this is a pretty grey area. It is clear that someone who has filled in their age as '183' has made a typo, and that you should not include this detail in your analysis. But what should you do if someone has a much slower response time than the other test subjects? From a statistical perspective, for example, there are ways to determine whether a data point is an **outlier**. When you clean up your data in a way that is beneficial to your conclusion, you may open yourself up to accusations of fraud. Be aware of this and check (with your lecturer) how far you can go when cleaning up your data. Before submitting your work, check once more whether you have been completely honest in displaying your research data and the clean-up method you have used. Disappointing research data say nothing about the quality of your research, but are part and parcel of scholarship.

Appendices

Appendix A
Sample literature review

Can human beings remain omnivorous?

**A comparison of the environmental impact
of an omnivorous diet and a vegetarian diet**

Student name

Student number	X
Module	**Academische writing skills** **(BSc, semester 1, year 1)**
Lecturer	Y
Number of words	2099
Date	Z

Background
to research

Abstract

With the growing world population, demand for food is rising. With this, consumption of meat will rise. This literature review investigates the environmental impact of a vegetarian diet in comparison to an omnivorous diet. In doing so, we first look at the impact of the different diets on land use. Subsequently, we consider the impact on water use. Diverse scientific sources show that more land is used and more deforestation occurs to produce food for an omnivorous diet than for a vegetarian diet. The research cited also suggests that the water footprint for an omnivorous diet is larger than that of a vegetarian diet. A change in human consumption behaviour is therefore needed, should we want to minimize the impact on the environment.

Main question

Sub-questions

Method
(literature
research)
and main
conclusions

Important
discussion point

= structural elements

= signalling words

= writing style

Introduction

Broad, attractively written opening

For over two million years, human beings have been eating animal and plant products (Gibbons, 2007). With the rise in the world's population comes the question of whether human beings can allow themselves to remain omnivorous, or whether we should shift to a vegetarian diet in order to save the environment.

The global population is currently growing by an average of 81 million people per year. In July 2013, there were 7.2 billion people in the world, 648 million more than in 2005. Even if the fertility rate keeps falling, by 2050 the world population will probably have reached 9.6 billion (United Nations, 2013). With the increase in the world's population, demand for food is also growing. According to the Food and Agriculture Organization (FAO), in the coming decades the production of basic foodstuffs will have to rise by 60% in order to meet the anticipated demand for food (FAO, 2013). This production will affect the environment. For example, a lot of water is needed to grow tomatoes, processing potatoes requires high amounts of energy, and cattle farming is a major cause of eutrophication (Foster et al., 2007).

Socially relevant research

Example

Short sentences

In 2013, global meat production grew by 1.4% to 308.2 million tons (FAO, 2013). Animal feed is needed in order to produce meat. This feed, such as soya or grain, has to be cultivated, and this has consequences for the environment. The impact is greater than it would be if we were to eat the soya or grain instead of the meat, for not all of the energy from this process goes into producing cattle. A number of kilos of soya or grain are needed in order to produce a kilo of meat. Changing our diet could therefore help to reduce the impact on the environment. That a non-vegetarian diet has a greater impact on the environment than a vegetarian diet is stated by Marlow et al. (2009), for instance, in one of a growing number of articles on this subject. 'From an environmental perspective, what someone chooses to eat makes the difference.'

Explanation + background info for important concepts (meat production, animal feed, energy value)

Social relevance (increasing number of publications on this)

In this literature review, we seek to answer the question: what is the difference in the environmental impact of a vegetarian versus an omnivorous diet? In order to answer this question, we look successively at the consequences for land use and water use.

Main question

Sub-question 1

Sub-question 2

Cattle farming, soya production, and land-use

In this section, we seek to answer the following sub-question: what are the consequences for land use of a vegetarian diet compared with those of an omnivorous diet? We do so by considering the impact of both diets according to a life-cycle analysis (LCA) applied to land use. Subsequently, to illustrate this impact, we discuss the situation in Brazil.

A lot of meat needs to be produced in order to meet the rising demand for food (FAO, 2013). The cattle industry needs land for meat production, whether for grazing cattle or for fields in which to cultivate cattle feed. This, in turn, has consequences for land use. In their research on the environmental impact of various diets, Baroni, Cenci, Tettamanti, and Berati (2007) used the LCA method. The LCA is a method whereby the environmental impact of a particular product (or combination of products) is established by looking at the whole life cycle, from raw material to waste (Agentschap NL, n.d.). They do this by considering various diets, including a diet containing meat and a vegetarian diet. The daily number of calories provided by the diets is almost identical. In addition, a distinction is made with respect to production: for both diets, the authors looked at the difference between the environmental impact of conventional and organic farming.

This research shows that when the same production method is used, a diet containing meat has the greatest impact on land use (Baroni et al., 2007). Around 1.5 times more land is needed to produce the average omnivorous organic diet than to produce a vegetarian organic diet.

According to Baroni et al. (2007), the great impact of an omnivorous diet is largely due to the land that is needed to cultivate cattle feed and for grazing. In their book *People of the tropical rain forest*, Denslow and Padoch (1988, cited in Baroni et al., 2007) refer to the link between the increasing use of land for cattle farming and deforestation. Forests are cleared to cultivate enough agricultural land, and in dry regions intensive agriculture can even lead to desertification (Christopherson & Birkeland, 2013).

Introduction to section

Jargon is avoided

Brazil is a good example of a country where deforestation is taking place for the cattle industry. In his research into the environmental impact of soya cultivation in Brazil, Fearnside (2001) states that 'Soybeans represent a recent and powerful threat to the biodiversity in Brazil' (p. 23). This soya is mostly exported to countries in Europe, where the soya is used as cattle feed. Many natural reserves are being lost to soya cultivation, including the Cerrado, grasslands, and the rain forests (Fearnside, 2001). In addition, major infrastructural development has taken place in order to transport the soya. The building of infrastructure in combination with the change in land use for plantations also has consequences for the soil. Soil degradation in the form of erosion is a major problem in Brazil, according to Fearnside (2001). Here we should mention that most, but not all, soya is used as cattle feed. Part of the soya is used for soya products that are consumed directly by humans.

Statement

Own comment

Most researchers agree that deforestation and soil degradation are taking place in Brazil, but they do not agree that soya plantations are the main cause of this. Barona, Ramankutty, Hyman, and Coomes (2010) investigated the role played by the expansion of the number of cattle farms in deforestation in Brazil. They compared the number of cattle farms with the link between deforestation and the expansion of the number of soya plantations between 2000 and 2006. From this, they concluded that the deforestation was primarily a result of cattle farming. It is the case, though, that part of the grazing land for cattle has had to make way for soya plantations, and the cattle farms have therefore had to shift to the rain forests.

It is clear that consuming a diet containing meat has more impact on land use than a vegetarian diet. The case of Brazil illustrates the consequences that the cattle farming industry has for land use. Whether caused by the expansion of agricultural land for soya cultivation or the expansion of grazing land for cattle, both are a consequence of growing meat consumption. In addition to land use, food production also has an impact on water use, and this will be discussed in the following section.

Conclusion

Sub-conclusion of section

Link to next section

Water use

In this section, we seek to answer the following sub-question: what are the consequences for water use of a vegetarian diet compared with those of an omnivorous diet? We do so by comparing the differences in water use for the production of meat and vegetables. Subsequently, we cite research into the water footprint of a soya burger and an equivalent product as an example of the impact on water use.

Sub-questions

The world's supply of fresh water is decreasing per head of the population, and this decrease has been linked to the global food shortage, among other things (Pimentel & Pimentel, 1993, cited in Baroni et al., 2007). Although Baroni et al. (2007) do not show how a vegetarian diet impacts water use in comparison to an omnivorous diet in their results, they do mention this as an important factor. The World Watch Institute (2004, cited in Baroni et al., 2007) investigated fresh water consumption worldwide.

Antithesis

Consequence

Accurate comparison

Antithesis

This research shows that 70% of all fresh water is used in cattle farming and agriculture, as opposed to just 22% by industry. It is mainly the cultivation of crops used for cattle feed that uses a lot of water. As a result, much more water is needed to produce a kilogram of meat than a kilogram of vegetables. Renault and Wallender (2000) investigated the quantity of water that is used to produce different sorts of feed. Their research shows that 4.3 m3 (4,300 litres) of water is needed to produce a kilogram of chicken or pork, whereas just 0.15 m3 (150 litres) of water is needed to produce a kilogram of vegetables.

Example

In the research by Ercin, Aldaya, and Hoesktra (2012), the water footprint is considered. In this footprint they include not only the water used in the entire production process, but also water pollution (Hoekstra & Mekonnen, 2012). Ercin et al. (2012) investigated the water footprint of a soya burger compared to that of a beef burger. The research considered every part of the production of the two burgers, each weighing 150 grams. The researchers not only looked at the footprint of the burgers' ingredients, but also, for example, at packaging material. In addition, the researchers looked at total water consumption for the water footprint: both surface and ground water and rain water, as well as the volume of water needed to bring contaminated water back to an acceptable norm. The research shows that the water footprint of a soya burger is much smaller than that of a beef burger. The water footprint of a beef burger is fourteen times larger than that of its vegetarian substitute.

Degree of probability

Antithesis

The above suggests that a vegetarian diet has a somewhat smaller impact on the fresh water supply than a diet containing meat. Whether one considers agriculture alone or the entire production chain makes little difference: the production of meat has a much larger impact on water use than the production of vegetables or meat substitutes.

Sub-conclusion

Conclusion and discussion

Answer to main question

The cited sources seem to support the claim that there are differences in the environmental impact of a diet containing meat and a non-meat diet. The consequences for land use are greater for an omnivorous diet than for a vegetarian diet. This is due to the amount of land that is needed for the cattle-farming industry, both for the cultivation of cattle feed and as a habitat for cattle. The consequences for water use are also greater when a diet containing meat is consumed. Much more water is needed to produce meat than to produce vegetables or meat substitutes. A vegetarian diet thus appears to have a smaller negative impact on the environment.

Answer to sub-questions
Cause
Conclusion

For this research, we chose to analyse particular regions (Brazil) and particular products (soya burgers). Although it is theoretically possible that completely different conclusions could be drawn for other regions and for other products, this appears unlikely. Cattle will always need feed and a habitat, and a number of kilos of plant material will always be needed to produce a single kilo of meat, because the conversion will never be 100% efficient.

Concession
Degree of probability
Reasons

The environment consists of more components than land and water, of course. In this research, we chose to look only at land use and water use, but food production also has other environmental effects. For example, this includes greenhouse gas emissions, the contamination of soil, air and water, the use of natural resources, substances that are harmful to human health, and the use of energy. These could be considered in future research.

Antithesis

Limitations of the research. This mainly adds nuance to the main and sub-questions, or at least puts conclusions in context.

There is also a third option, besides a diet containing meat and a vegetarian diet: that of a vegan diet. After all, certain animal products are included in a vegetarian diet, such as eggs and milk. Cattle farming is still needed to produce these, though to a lesser degree. Baroni et al. (2007) did consider this diet, and their research does indeed suggest that a vegan diet would be even better for the environment.

Instead of adjusting our own consumption behaviour, it would also be possible to make changes to cattle feed. Elferink, Nonhebel, and Moll (2008) have researched the possibility of using waste as cattle feed. This would reduce the environmental impact of meat somewhat, and would be another interesting direction to explore in future research.

Suggestions for further research

It is clear that as the world's population grows, we will no longer be able to keep consuming in our present fashion. This does not mean that we will have to stop eating meat altogether. If we want to minimize our impact on the environment, though, meat consumption per head will have to fall. Can human beings remain omnivorous? For the time being, we can, but in moderation.

Short, snappy conclusion with an attractive ending and a link back to the beginning

Bibliography

Agentschap NL. (n.d.). *Levens Cyclus Analyse (LCA)*. Retrieved on November 17 2013 from http://www.agentschapnl.nl/onderwerpen/duurzaam-ondernemen/ starten-met-duurzaam-ondernemen/duurzaam-productontwerp/ levens-cyclus-analyse

Barona, E., Ramankutty, N., Hyman, G. & Coomes, O.T. (2010). The role of pasture and soybean in deforestation of the Brazilian Amazon. *Environmental Research Letters, 5*(2), 1-9. doi:10.1088/1748-9326/5/2/024002

Baroni, L., Cenci, L., Tettamanti, M. & Berati, M. (2006). Evaluating the environmental impact of various dietary patterns combined with different food production systems. *European Journal of Clinical Nutrition, 61*(2), 279-286. doi:10.1038/sj.ejcn.1602522

Christopherson, R.W. & Birkeland, G. (2013). *Elemental geosystems*. Glenview: Pearson Education, Inc.

Elferink, E.V., Nonhebel, S. & Moll, H.C. (2008). Feeding livestock food residue and the consequences for the environmental impact of meat. *Journal of Cleaner Production, 16*(12), 1227-1233. doi:10.1016/j.jclepro.2007.06.008

Ercin, A.E., Aldaya, M.M. & Hoekstra, A.Y. (2012). The water footprint of soy milk and soy burger and equivalent animal products. *Ecological Indicators, 18*, 392-402. doi:10.1016/j.ecolind.2011.12.009

Fearnside, P.M. (2001). Soybean cultivation as a threat to the environment in Brazil. *Environmental Conservation, 28*(1), 23-38. Retrieved from https://faculty. washington.edu/jhannah/geog270aut07/readings/GreenGeneRevolutions/ Fearnside%20-%20SoybeanCultivationThreatEnvironment.pdf

Food and Agriculture Organization. (2013). *The state of food and agriculture 2013*. Retrieved from http://www.fao.org/docrep/018/i3300e/i3300e.pdf

Foster, C., Green, K., Bleda, M., Dewick, P., Evans, B., Flynn, A. & Mylan, J. (2007). *Environmental impacts of food production and consumption: A report to the Department for Environment Food and Rural Affairs*. London: Manchester Business School.

Gibbons, A. (2007). Food for thought. *Science, 316*(5831), 1558-1560.

Hoekstra, A.Y. & Mekonnen, M.M. (2012). The water footprint of humanity. *Proceedings of the National Academy of Sciences, 109*(9), 3232-3237. doi:10.1073/ pnas.1109936109

Marlow, H.J., Hayes, W.K., Soret, S., Carter, R.L., Schwab, E.R. & Sabaté, J. (2009). Diet and the environment: does what you eat matter?. *The American journal of clinical nutrition, 89*(5), 1699S-1703S. doi:10.3945/ajcn.2009.26736Z

Renault, D., & Wallender, W. W., (2000). Nutritional water productivity and diets. *Agricultural Water Management, 45*(3), 275-296.

United Nations, Department of Economic and Social Affairs, Population Division. (2013). *World Population Prospects: The 2012 Revision, Highlights and Advance Tables*. Retrieved on 17 November 2013 from http://esa.un.org/unpd/wpp/ Documentation/pdf/WPP2012_HIGHLIGHTS.pdf

Citation: research article

Citation: book

Citation: report

Appendix B
Sample research article

Cannabis-users have stronger attentional bias for cannabis cues. This is related to problematic cannabis use, but not due to a general defect in cognitive control.

Abstract

It is possible that individuals with a high level of cognitive control are more successful in suppressing a stronger attentional bias for drug cues and thereby run a lower risk of problematic drug use. The present study will examine this relationship. This was investigated by administering the cannabis Stroop task (stronger attentional bias for cannabis cues) and the classical Stroop task (cognitive control) in a group of heavy cannabis users (N=26) and a matched control group (N=26). The severity of cannabis use was measured using the CUDIT. The scores for the cannabis Stroop task were significantly higher in the cannabis group than the control group, but the scores for the classical Stroop task were equal between the groups. Within the cannabis group, there was a positive correlation between the score for the CUDIT and the cannabis Stroop task. In other words, the attentional bias for cannabis words was higher in the cannabis group than in the control group, but the cognitive control scores were the same. This suggests that cannabis users have stronger attentional bias for cannabis cues and that this is not due to a general defect in cognitive control, but related to problematic cannabis use. These findings supplement knowledge regarding cannabis use and may have implications for policymakers.

This sample report is based on the article:
Cousijn, J., Watson, P., Koenders, L., Vingerhoets, W.A.M., Goudriaan, A.E., & Wiers, R.W. (2013). Cannabis dependence, cognitive control and attentional bias for cannabis words. *Addictive Behaviors, 38*, 2825-2832. Doi: https://doi.org/10.1016/j.addbeh.2013.08.011

Introduction

Theoretical framework on attentional bias

The influential incentive sensitization model of addiction proposes that drug addiction arises because the brain is sensitized by the use of a drug. This means that someone who repeatedly uses drugs in the same environment becomes hypersensitive to factors in this environment (Robinson & Berridge, 1993). These environmental factors become drug cues, which strongly and automatically attract this person's attention (see Field and Cox, 2008, for a review). This leads to craving for the drugs, which again increases the likelihood of reuse (Robinson & Berridge, 1993, 2000, 2001). Indeed, previous research has shown that increased attention for drug cues is related to craving (see Field, Munafò and Franken, 2009, for a meta-analysis), relapse into use, and escalation of drugs-related problems (Carpenter, Schreiber, Church, & McDowell, 2006; Marhe, Waters, van de Wetering, & Franken, 2013; Waters, Marhe, & Franken, 2012).

Problem statement: social relevance

This shows that investigating increased attention for drug cues is an important behavioural indicator of problematic drug use.

Theoretical framework on cognitive control

In addition to the automatic, increased attention for drug cues, which increase the chance of drug use, there is a conscious cognitive control system that can suppress this tendency (Hofmann, Friese, & Strack, 2009; Stacy & Wiers, 2010; Wiers et al., 2007). Cognitive control can be defined as the effective use of attention and memory processes, among other things, whereby behaviour can be modified flexibly (Botvinick, Braver, Barch, Carter, & Cohen, 2001; Ridderinkhof, Ullsperger, Crone, & Nieuwenhuis, 2004).

Theoretical framework: relationship between cognitive control and attentional bias

It is possible that individuals with a high level of cognitive control are more successful in suppressing the stronger attentional bias for drug cues and thereby run a lower risk of problematic drug use.

Problem statement: scientific relevance

However, this has not previously been researched.

Research question

The current study therefore examines the relationship between cognitive control, attentional bias for drug cues and problematic drug use.

Hypothesis

The hypothesis is that the relationship between stronger attentional bias for drug cues and cannabis use is dependent on the degree of cognitive control.

Setup

Attentional bias for drug cues was measured using the cannabis Stroop task (Cox, Fadardi, & Pothos, 2006). Cognitive control was measured using the classical version of the Stroop task (Stroop, 1935). Both were administered in a group of heavy cannabis users and a matched control group.

Predictions

Based on previous research (Cane, Sharma, & Albery, 2009; Field, 2005), the expectation was that the cannabis users would have stronger attentional bias for the cannabis words in comparison to the neutral words, whereas this would not be the case for the participants from the control group. In addition, it was expected that this would not be a result of overall cognitive problems, and that this stronger attentional bias for cannabis words would be related to cannabis use and cannabis dependence.

Method

Participants

The participants in the study were 26 heavy cannabis users and 26 participants who never or hardly ever use cannabis (the control group), matched by age and gender. All participants were aged between 18 and 30 years (see Table 1 for information about the sample). All participants were recruited via online adverts. Cannabis users were included if they had been using on a weekly basis for at least two years and had never been treated for cannabis addiction. Participants in the control group were included if they had not used any cannabis in the last month and had used cannabis fewer than 50 times over their lives. Participants were excluded if they had a physical or psychiatric disorder. The study was approved by the ethics committee of the Academic Medical Centre in Amsterdam (AMC) and all participants signed an informed consent form.

Materials

Demographic information about the sample was obtained by means of a generic questionnaire, in which questions were also asked about cannabis use. The eight-item Cannabis Use Identification Test (CUDIT; Adamson et al., 2010) was used to obtain information about the severity of use and possible problems arising from cannabis use. The CUDIT scores run from 0 to 32. Ninety-one per cent of patients who have cannabis use disorders (cannabis abuse or addiction) score higher than 13 (Adamson et al., 2010).

Cognitive control was measured using the validated Dutch version of the classical Stroop task (Hammes, 1971). This test consisted of three subtests. For the first subtest, one hundred words were printed on a sheet of paper in random order. These were the words 'blue', 'green', 'red', and 'yellow' printed in black ink. The participants had to read out loud what they could see as quickly as they could. In the second subtest, one hundred coloured squares were printed on the sheet, in the colours blue, green, red, and yellow. This time, the participants had to name the colour of the ink as quickly as possible. In the third subtest, the four words 'blue', 'green', 'red', and 'yellow' were printed in coloured ink. The colour of the ink was incongruous with the meaning of the word (for example, the word 'blue' was printed in yellow ink). The cognitive control was calculated based on the time taken to carry out the various sub-tasks (the average of the first two sub-tasks was deducted from the time taken to carry out the third sub-task). A high score is an indication of interference and therefore of low cognitive control.

The attentional bias for cannabis words was measured using the cannabis Stroop task (Cox et al., 2006). The test consisted of two subtests. The first subtest consisted of fourteen words related to cannabis use that were printed four times on a sheet of paper in random order, in coloured ink (blue, red, yellow, and green). The second subtest was identical, but consisted of fourteen random neutral words in coloured ink.

The participants had to say the name of the colour of the ink out loud. The measure of attention was calculated by deducting the time taken to read out the neutral words from the time taken to read out the cannabis words. A positive score is an indication of interference due to the meaning of the words, and thereby indicates a stronger attentional bias for cannabis words.

Procedure
Participants gave their informed consent in writing. The cannabis Stroop task was administered first, alternately beginning with subtest 1 or subtest 2. The classical Stroop task was subsequently administered, whereby the three sub-tasks were always administered in the same order (1, 2, and 3). Finally, the demographic questions were asked and the CUDIT was administered.

Statistical analysis
The demographic data were compared using independent t-tests and the male/female proportions with an χ^2-test. The scores for the attentional bias for cannabis words and the cognitive control were compared between the cannabis group and the control group using independent t-tests. Within the cannabis group, the researchers looked at whether there was a relationship between the attentional bias for cannabis words and problematic cannabis use, as measured with the CUDIT. This was done by means of a Pearson correlation test.

Results

Both the cannabis use and the CUDIT scores were significantly higher in the cannabis group than in the control group, and there was no significant difference between the average ages of the two groups (Table 1). The proportion of women was similar within the cannabis group (23%) and the control group (35%, $\chi^2(1) = 0.84$, $p = 0.36$).

Descriptive statistics

Comparative statistics

On average, the attentional bias for cannabis words was significantly higher in the cannabis group (M 2.04, SD = 3.52) than in the control group (M = -0.73, SD = 3.96, $t(50) = 2.68$, $p \leq 0.01$, Figure 1). By contrast, the scores for cognitive control were similar between the cannabis group (M = 32.71, SD = 10.86) and the control group (M = 31.58, SD = 15.71, $t(50) = 0.30$, $p = 0.76$). Within the cannabis group, the researchers found a positive correlation for stronger attentional bias for cannabis words and the score on the CUDIT ($r = 0.48$, $p = 0.01$, Figure 2).

Table 1 Information about the sample of 26 cannabis users, six of whom are women (23%), and 26 control users, nine of whom are women (35%)

	Cannabis group (N=26)		Control group (N=26)		Statistical values	
	Average	Standard Deviation	Average	Standard Deviation	Test statistic	p-value
Age (years)	21.44	2.50	22.14	2.48	$t(50) = -1.02$	$p = 0.31$
Cannabis use per week (g)	3.33	4.25	0.02	0.10	$t(25) = 3.97$	$p \leq 0.01$
CUDIT score*	12.42	6.00	0.04	0.20	$t(25) = 10.51$	$p \leq 0.01$

*CUDIT=Cannabis Use Disorders Identification Test

Figure 1 Attentional bias for cannabis words was significantly higher in the cannabis group than in the control group

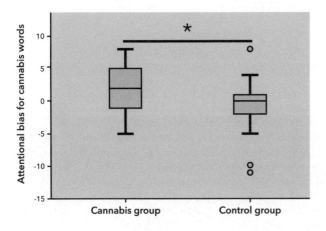

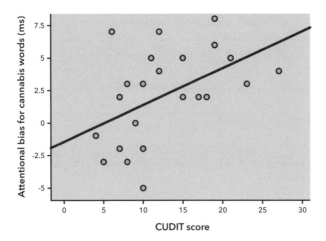

Figure 2 Within the cannabis group, a significant positive correlation was found between the degree of problematic cannabis use (CUDIT score) and the attentional bias for cannabis words

Discussion

Summary of results

The objective of this study was to investigate the relationship between cognitive control, stronger attentional bias for drug cues, and problematic drug use. It was found that the group of cannabis users showed a stronger attentional bias for cannabis words compared to the group of healthy control group. In addition, we found that the cognitive control of cannabis users was similar to that of the healthy control group. It was also found that within the group of cannabis users, the stronger attentional bias for cannabis words was related to more problematic cannabis use.

Conclusion

In conclusion: in the present study, no differences in cognitive control were found, but a difference was found in attentional bias for cannabis cues between the cannabis group and the control group.

Evaluation: finding on attentional bias for cannabis cues

This suggests that cannabis users have a stronger attentional bias for cannabis cues, which is not due to a general defect in cognitive control, but related to problematic cannabis use. The same relationship between stronger attentional bias for drug cues and drug-use problems (dependence and use) has been demonstrated for different sorts of drugs, including alcohol, nicotine, heroin, and cocaine (Field, 2005; Field & Cox, 2008; Hester, Dixon & Garavan, 2006). The stronger attentional bias for cannabis cues replicates the findings of Cane et al. (2009).

The hypothesis investigated in this study was that individuals with a high degree of cognitive control would be more successful in suppressing the stronger attentional bias for drug cues, and thereby run a lower risk of problematic drug use. This has been found in various studies that examine this relationship in alcohol cues (Friese, Bargas-Avila, Hofmann & Wiers, 2010; Grenard et al., 2008; Peeters et al., 2012). However, our results do not support this hypothesis. This could be because the majority of the cannabis users in our sample did not have a diagnosis of cannabis dependence. Only 38% (just ten participants) of the cannabis users had a CUDIT score of 13 or more, which can be seen as a clinical diagnosis of cannabis dependence. It is therefore possible that we had insufficient statistical power to be able to investigate the modulating role of cognitive control. Follow-up research should thus include a sample with a sufficient number of dependent cannabis users.

Evaluation: relationship between cognitive control, attentional bias for drug cues, and drug use

Limitation

Suggestion for follow-up research

Although the present study can only speculate about causality, Waters et al. (2012) reported that heroin and cocaine addicts had a stronger attentional bias for heroin and cocaine cues just before craving arose and the participants experienced a relapse in use. In addition, there are studies that have attempted to manipulate this stronger attentional bias for drug cues through training, in order to influence drug use. This has been done for alcohol addiction, for example, where it was indeed found that lowering attentional bias for alcohol cues led to a lessening of relapse in alcohol use (Fadardi & Cox, 2009; Schoenmakers et al., 2010). The same was found for nicotine addiction (Attwood, O'Sullivan, Leonards, Mackintosh, & Munafò, 2008). In view of the importance of attentional bias for drug cues in the process of addiction and the possibility of influencing this, this remains an extremely important topic for follow-up research.

The participants included in the cannabis group were all heavy cannabis users. However, just 38% of the cannabis users had a CUDIT score of 13 or more, which can be seen as a clinical diagnosis of cannabis dependence. This shows that heavy use is not necessarily accompanied by dependence problems. In addition, in this study, heavy use was not found to have a negative effect on cognitive control. These findings add to our knowledge on cannabis use and may have implications for policymakers (see also Advisory Council on the Misuse of Drugs [ACMD], 2003). In conclusion, heavy cannabis users have a stronger attentional bias for cannabis cues, but this is not due to a general defect in cognitive control.

Implication for practice

Conclusion

Bibliography

Adamson, S.J., Kay-Lambkin, F.J., Baker, A.L., Lewin, T.J., Thornton, L., Kelly, B.J., et al. (2010). An improved brief measure of cannabis misuse: The Cannabis Use Disorders Identification Test – Revised (CUDIT-R). *Drug and Alcohol Dependence, 110*(1-2), 137-143. Doi: https://doi.org/10.1016/j.drugalcdep.2010.02.017

Advisory Council on the Misuse of Drugs. (2003). *The Classification of Cannabis under the Misuse of Drugs Act 1971.* London: Home Office.

Attwood, A.S., O'Sullivan, H., Leonards, U., Mackintosh, B., & Munafò, M.R. (2008). Attentional bias training and cue reactivity in cigarette smokers. *Addiction, 103*(11), 1875-1882. Doi: https://doi.org/10.1111/j.1360-0443.2008.02335.x

Botvinick, M.M., Braver, T.S., Barch, D.M., Carter, C.S., & Cohen, J.D. (2001). Conflict monitoring and cognitive control. *Psychological Review, 108*(3), 624-652. Doi: https://doi.org/10.1037/0033-295X.108.3.624

Cane, J.E., Sharma, D., & Albery, I.P. (2009). The addiction Stroop task: Examining the fast and slow effects of smoking and marijuana-related cues. *Journal of Psychopharmacology, 23*(5), 510-519. Doi: https://doi.org/10.1177/0269881108091253

Carpenter, K.M., Schreiber, E., Church, S., & McDowell, D. (2006). Drug Stroop performance: Relationships with primary substance of use and treatment outcome in a drug-dependent outpatient sample. *Addictive Behaviors, 31*(1), 174-181. Doi: https://doi.org/10.1016/j.addbeh.2005.04.012

Cox, W.M., Fadardi, J.S., & Pothos, E.M. (2006). The addiction-Stroop test: Theoretical considerations and procedural recommendations. *Psychological Bulletin, 132*(3), 443-476. Doi: https://doi.org/10.1037/0033-2909.132.3.443

Fadardi, J.S., & Cox, W.M. (2009). Reversing the sequence: Reducing alcohol consumption by overcoming alcohol attentional bias. *Drug and Alcohol Dependence, 101*(3), 137-145.

Field, M. (2005). Cannabis 'dependence' and attentional bias for cannabis-related words. *Behavioural Pharmacology, 16*(5-6), 473-476. Doi: https://doi.org/10.1016/j.drugalcdep.2008.11.015

Field, M., & Cox, W.M. (2008). Attentional bias in addictive behaviors: A review of its development, causes, and consequences. *Drug and Alcohol Dependence, 97*(1-2), 1-20. DOi: https://doi.org/10.1016/j.drugalcdep.2008.03.030

Field, M., Munafò, M.R., & Franken, I.H.A. (2009). A meta-analytic investigation of the relationship between attentional bias and subjective craving in substance abuse. *Psychological Bulletin, 135*(4), 589-607. Doi: https://doi.org/10.1037/a0015843

Friese, M., Bargas-Avila, J., Hofmann, W., & Wiers, R.W. (2010). Here's looking at you, bud: Alcohol-related memory structures predict eye movements for social drinkers with low executive control. *Social Psychological and Personality Science, 1*(2), 143-151. Doi: https://doi.org/10.1177/1948550609359945

Grenard, J.L., Ames, S.L., Wiers, R.W., Thush, C., Sussman, S., & Stacy, A.W. (2008). Working memory capacity moderates the predictive effects of drug-related associations on substance use. *Psychology of Addictive Behaviors: Journal of the Society of Psychologists in Addictive Behaviors, 22*(3), 426-432. Doi: https://doi.org/10.1037/0893-164X.22.3.426

Hammes, J.G.W. (1971). *De Stroop Kleur-Woord Test. Handleiding.* Lisse: Swets & Zeitlinger.

Hester, R., Dixon, V., & Garavan, H. (2006). A consistent attentional bias for drug-related material in active cocaine users across word and picture versions of the emotional Stroop task. *Drug and Alcohol Dependence, 81*(3), 251-257. Doi: https://doi.org/10.1016/j.drugalcdep.2005.07.002

Hofmann, W., Friese, M., & Strack, F. (2009). Impulse and self-control from a dual-systems perspective. *Perspectives on Psychological Science, 4*(2), 162-176. Doi: https://doi.org/10.1111/j.1745-6924.2009.01116.x

Marhe, R., Waters, A.J., Van de Wetering, B.J.M., & Franken, I.H.A. (2013). Implicit and explicit drug-related cognitions during detoxification treatment are associated with drug relapse: An ecological momentary assessment study. *Journal of Consulting and Clinical Psychology, 81*(1), 1-12. Doi: https://doi.org/10.1037/a0030754

Peeters, M., Wiers, R.W., Monshouwer, K., Van de Schoot, R., Janssen, T., & Vollebergh, W.A.M. (2012). Automatic processes in at-risk adolescents: The role of alcohol-approach tendencies and response inhibition in drinking behavior. *Addiction, 107*(11), 1939-1946. Doi: https://doi.org/10.1111/j.1360-0443.2012.03948.x

Ridderinkhof, K.R., Ullsperger, M., Crone, E.A., & Nieuwenhuis, S. (2004). The role of the medial frontal cortex in cognitive control. *Science, 306*(5695), 443-447. Doi: https://doi.org/10.1126/science.1100301

Robinson, T.E., & Berridge, K.C. (1993). The neural basis of drug craving: An incentive-sensitization theory of addiction. *Brain Research Reviews, 18*(3), 247-291. Doi: https://doi.org/10.1016/0165-0173(93)90013-P

Robinson, T.E., & Berridge, K.C. (2000). The psychology and neurobiology of addiction: An incentive-sensitization view. *Addiction, 95*(Suppl. 2), S91-S117. Doi: https://doi.org/10.1080/09652140050111681

Robinson, T.E., & Berridge, K.C. (2001). Incentive-sensitization and addiction. *Addiction, 96*(1), 103-114. Doi: https://doi.org/10.1080/09652140020016996

Schoenmakers, T.M., De Bruin, M., Lux, I.F.M., Goertz, A.G., Van Kerkhof, D.H.A.T., & Wiers, R.W. (2010). Clinical effectiveness of attentional bias modification training in abstinent alcoholic patients. *Drug and Alcohol Dependence, 109*(1-3), 30-36. Doi: https://doi.org/10.1016/j.drugalcdep.2009.11.022

Stacy, A.W., & Wiers, R.W. (2010). Implicit cognition and addiction: A tool for explaining paradoxical behavior. *Annual Review of Clinical Psychology, 6*, 551-575. Doi: https://doi.org/10.1146/annurev.clinpsy.121208.131444

Stroop, R.J. (1935). Studies of interference in serial verbal reactions. *Journal of Experimental Psychology, 18*(6), 643-662. Doi: https://doi.org/10.1037/h0054651

Waters, A.J., Marhe, R., & Franken, I.H.A. (2012). Attentional bias to drug cues is elevated before and during temptations to use heroin and cocaine. *Psychopharmacology, 219*(3), 909-921. Doi: https://doi.org/10.1007/s00213-011-2424-z

Wiers, R.W., Bartholow, B.D., Van Den Wildenberg, E., Thush, C., Engels, R.C.M.E., Sher, K.J., et al. (2007). Automatic and controlled processes and the development of addictive behaviors in adolescents: A review and a model. Pharmacology Biochemistry and Behavior, 86(2), 263-283. Doi: https://doi.org/10.1016/j.pbb.2006.09.021

Colophon

University of Amsterdam

The University of Amsterdam (UvA), with some 30,000 students, 5,000 staff, and a budget of more than 600 million euros, is one of the largest comprehensive universities in Europe. Teaching and research at the UvA are conducted at seven faculties: the Humanities, Social and Behavioural Sciences, Economics and Business, Law, Science, and Medicine and Dentistry, with programs offered in almost every field.

The Institute for Interdisciplinary Studies

The Institute for Interdisciplinary Studies (IIS) is a knowledge center for interdisciplinary learning and teaching. Each year, the institute provides a diversity of interdisciplinary education to some 3,300 students enrolled in bachelor's or master's programs or open courses. In recent years, dozens of lecturers in different disciplines from within and outside the UvA have contributed to education or other activities in the institute. The Institute is a 'laboratory' for interdisciplinary experiments and projects that might lead to new interdisciplinary courses, teaching methods, or programs. The IIS conducts assignments and projects for clients both within and outside the UvA. It also advises on interdisciplinary education.

Contact

Institute for Interdisciplinary Studies
Science Park 904
1098 XH Amsterdam
Tel. +31 20 525 51 90
www.iis.uva.nl
Onderwijslab-iis@uva.nl

Also published in the Series Perspectives on Interdiscipinarity:

Academic Skills for Interdisciplinary Studies. Revised Edition (2019). Koen van der Gaast, Laura Koenders and Ger Post

Academische vaardigheden voor interdisciplinaire studies. Vierde, herziene druk (2019). Koen van der Gaast, Laura Koenders en Ger Post

Designing Interdisciplinary Education. A Practical Handbook for University Teachers (2017). Linda de Greef, Ger Post, Christianne Vink and Lucy Wenting

Interdisciplinary Learning Activities (2018). Hannah Edelbroek, Myrte Mijnders, and Ger Post

Wicked Philosophy. Philosophy of Science and Vision Development for Complex Problems (2018). Coyan Tromp